Our Quirky
Guide *to* Seattle

Our Quirky Guide *to* Seattle

BY VARIOUS CONTRIBUTORS

P.O. Box 400818
Las Vegas, NV 89140

ISBN-13: 9781439286777
ISBN-10: 1439286779

Dedication

We would like to dedicate this book to our dear friend Holly. Our thoughts are with you during this difficult time, and we wish you a speedy recovery. We look forward to sharing many more experiences with you soon in our unique city of Seattle.

Introduction

We're not travel experts. Rather, we're a group of friends and coworkers, a bit ambitious and a bit peculiar, who enjoy our time with each other and enjoy partaking in what Seattle has to offer. We work hard, and it leaves us little time to play. We try to maximize our limited leisure time by pursuing our passions, going to places we love, and having fun.

This is not a complete book of Seattle activities. Instead, it is a collection of our favorite activities. You will find a full range of arts, dining, outdoor, and travel suggestions. Perhaps one of our favorites will become one of yours.

The forty-two of us were able to come together, collaborate, and create a book. This was possible only through the flexibility of self-publishing.

We feel fortunate to live in Seattle. It is a place that is always raining, just finished raining, or is about to rain. It makes us appreciate our time outdoors and the beautiful scenery even more. We hope our words will help you explore, taste, smell, feel, and hear all things Seattle.

Contributors:

Adria Meno

Alan Kipust

Atif Rafiq

Balaji Nageswaran

Benjamin Tucker

Bhushan Shah

Brent Fattore

Brianne Kwasny

Brittany Goode

Brittany Turner

Brynn Duke

Clover Kim

Cynthia Prentice

David Azari

David Keys

David Leatham

Dirk Vogel

Duncan Sherrard

Emily Tyack

Gabriela Franc

Holly Zimmerman

James Kirchmer

Josh Wright

Katy Ardans

Kelly Watson

Krsevan Penzar

Lee Miller

Luciana Bodily

Malissa Kent

Marc Miller

Martina Mett

Mary Beth Zaccari

Nader Kabbani

Neil Critchley

Nick Hebb

Rod Learmonth

Stephanie Franklin

Tanvi Bhadbhade

Theresa Hollis

Tony Martinelli

Uday Kumar Kollu

Contents

EATING OUT

LEGEND
Price Per Plate
$ < 10
$$ 11–19
$$$ 20–29
$$$$ > 30
Local = Sources Ingredients Locally
♻ = Eco-Friendly
V = Vegetarian-Friendly

BAKERIES AND COFFEE SHOPS

CAFÉ BESALU $ **Local** V
5909 24th Ave. NW, Seattle, WA 98107
(206) 789-1463
WED–SUN 6:00 a.m.–3:00 p.m.
www.cafebesalu.com

Drive past Café Besalu on any given morning and you will quickly notice the line outside the unassuming storefront on a quiet street in Ballard. The lines start early and last well throughout the morning, all for the chance to stand in front of the single display case and order some of the best croissants and pastries in Seattle. The croissants themselves are the gold standard, quite possibly the best found outside of France and most certainly the best in Seattle. They are flaky, buttery, airy, and pair perfectly with the homemade jams served on the side. The house specialty is the almond croissant, which takes the delicious regular croissant and adds an almond center that is not too overpowering or too sweet.

On top of the croissants, there is a collection of pastries focused on local and fresh ingredients. Typical mornings may include Danishes with apples, strawberries, or plums, which are set atop a fresh pastry and a humble but delicious vanilla cream. Not to be overlooked are the other baked goods that line the bottom shelf such as lemon cookies, coconut macaroons, baked cardamom pretzels (our favorite), or sample one of the quiches that line the top of the display case.

On the weekends, don't expect to find seating in the small dining room with only ten to twelve tables, but instead opt to take your treats to one of the many local parks to enjoy.

Insider tip—head over in the early afternoon and beat the lines. The pastries are continually updated throughout the day and are just as good as an afternoon snack with a latte.

FLYING APRON $$ Local ♦ V

3510 Fremont Ave. N., Seattle, WA 98103
(206) 442-1115
MON–WED 7:00 a.m.–7:00 p.m.
THU–SUN 7:00 a.m.–8:00 p.m.
www.flyingapron.com

It would be easy to walk right past the Flying Apron, situated in the heart of Fremont, just a block north of the bridge—but it would be a mistake. This little hole in the wall bakery/coffee shop is crammed full of delicious indulgences, 100% vegan and 100% gluten free. You might be skeptical about the sorts of pastries that are wheat, egg, and butter free, but the Flying Apron motto sums it up spectacularly: "It's not about what you *can't* eat." From drool-worthy cupcakes and cookies to sumptuous cakes, blondies, brownies, and scones, this bakery would satisfy even the most skeptical and discerning sweet tooth. The cinnamon rolls, made with garbanzo flour and chopped pecans, are phenomenal! The lemon poppy seed muffins would brighten any dreary Monday morning.

And the Flying Apron doesn't stop at sweets. There are a limited number of savory offerings and daily salads to choose from as well—the mini pizzas, either warmed or chilled, are always a pleasure. If you're not in the mood for a nibble, the Apron also serves a variety of teas, including a delicious yerba mate blend, and their coffee tastes as good as it smells. So the next time you're stuck waiting for that pesky bridge to close, hop out of traffic and treat yourself.

Macrina Bakery and Café $ V

Macrina (Belltown)
2408 First Ave., Seattle, WA 98121
(206) 448-4032
MON–SUN 7:00 a.m.–6:00 p.m.
www.macrinabakery.com

and
Macrina (McGraw)
615 W. McGraw St., Seattle, WA 98119

(206) 283-5900
MON–SUN 7:00 a.m.–6:00 p.m.

and

Macrina (SoDo)
1943 First Ave. S., Seattle, WA 98134
(206) 623-0919
MON–FRI 7:00 a.m.–6:00 p.m.
SAT 8:00 a.m.–5:00 p.m.
SUN 8:00 a.m.–3:00 p.m.

With three locations in Belltown, McGraw, and SoDo, Macrina is one of the best bakeries/cafés in the area. Anyone who is a sucker for delicious carbohydrates will appreciate Macrina's breads and pastries. There's an array of breads ranging from the Macrina Casera (house bread) to a brioche. Our personal favorite is the olivetta—a focaccia-like creation with green olives. Macrina also has a variety of pastries and cookies—from muffins to coffee cakes to cookies—and their menu of cake creations is mouthwatering. Call me boring, but my favorite sweet is Olivia's Chocolate Chip Cookies. This is by far the best chocolate chip cookie I've ever eaten. (Don't tell Mom!)

In addition to their bakery, Macrina has a café serving a variety of foods for breakfast, brunch, and lunch. The menu utilizes fresh, in-house baked bread to create delicious sandwiches. Couple that with a crisp salad of organic field greens, roasted red onions, olives, and almonds tossed with a balsamic vinaigrette, and you have a great lunch. Most recently, I had the bialy egg sandwich. I consider myself to be somewhat of an egg-sandwich connoisseur, and this one takes the cake for most decadently delicious combination of ingredients: two fried eggs, basil, goat cheese, Dijon mustard, tomato, and bacon (optional) all on top of a bakery fresh bialy roll.

Whether you're just grabbing food on the go or intending to sit and enjoy, Macrina is a great place if you've got a hankering for bread, pastries, or a delicious meal involving both.

Voxx $ V

2245 Eastlake Ave. E., Seattle, WA 98102
(206) 324-2778
MON–FRI 6:00 a.m.–10:00 p.m.
SAT–SUN 7:00 a.m.–10:00 p.m.
www.voxxseattle.com

Everyone knows Seattle is famous for its coffee. Being the *Twin Peaks* fan that I am, I embarked on the search for Washington State's "damn fine cup of coffee" shortly after moving to the Pacific Northwest. It just so happened that I moved into the Eastlake District, not far from Voxx Café.

This cozy café has an abundance of outlets, so you can plug in and surf the Web while sipping on a latte made with fair-trade, organic Stumptown coffee. I took one sip of the Hairbender latte and was convinced that this was the same coffee Agent Cooper must have had when he exclaimed, "This is, excuse me, a DAMN FINE cup of coffee!"

Voxx also offers a small variety of sandwiches, burritos, and doughnuts from local bakeries. I recommend one of their breakfast burritos or grilled sandwiches. They also offer Mighty-O doughnuts for vegans with a sweet tooth.

So if you're also in search of a damn fine cup of coffee or a relaxing atmosphere to get some work done or catch up on your e-mail, Voxx is the cream of the crop!

OUTDOOR DINING

AGUA VERDE CAFÉ $–$$ **V**
1303 NE Boat St., Seattle, WA 98105
(206) 545-8570
SUN–SAT 11:00 a.m.–3:30 p.m., 4:00 p.m.–9:00 p.m.
www.aguaverde.com/cafe.shtml

Agua Verde Café offers economical, vegan, and gluten-free Mexican cuisine, with several organic options on the menu. Menu items of note include the Mangodilla, a quesadilla made with Mexican mangoes, Jack cheese, poblano chilies, and scallions, and the Vegetariano, a vegetarian burrito that includes unique ingredients such as sautéed organic yams. Agua Verde also boasts some of the best organic tortilla chips. A self-serve salsa cart bar includes fresh salsa options (with varying spice levels) to accompany any meal.

Agua Verde also offers authentic Mexican beverages, including a variety of margaritas. Some noteworthy nonalcoholic beverages include Jarritos bottled Mexican sodas, Mexican chai, and chicha de piña (a pineapple, lemon, and lime juice).

The café has patio seating with great views of the Portage Bay. Patrons can also rent kayaks from the paddle club on the lower level, and there is ample street parking, though parking can get challenging when there is a University of Washington sports event.

Agua Verde is an economical and healthy combination of savory Mexican eats.

PASEO $

6226 Seaview Ave. NW, Seattle, WA 98117
(206) 789-3100
TUE–SAT 11:00 a.m.–8:00 p.m.
www.paseoseattle.com

and

4225 Fremont Ave. N., Seattle, WA 98103
(206) 545-7440
TUE–FRI 11:00 a.m.–9:00 p.m.
SAT 11:00 a.m.–8:00 p.m.

A few things to remember to ensure a great experience when eating at Paseo: 1) don't forget the cash (no credit cards accepted), 2) they are closed during the entire month of January, and 3) don't wear anything you are afraid to get messy. This Caribbean restaurant's two locations in Fremont and Ballard have drawn much acclaim both locally and nationally, and their delicious food is hardly a secret. The main attraction is the Cuban roast pork sandwich, which is marinated and slow roasted until it can be shredded and put atop a bun and smothered in mouthwatering aioli, cilantro, pickled jalapenos, and caramelized onions. The sandwiches are not dainty, and your hands will certainly be covered by the time you finish the sandwich.

Besides the roast, Paseo serves other succulent sandwiches like the Smokin' Chicken Thighs, Sautéed Prawns, and the Midnight Cuban Press, which tops the roast pork with ham, Swiss cheese, and sweet banana peppers and then presses it all. Even at this temple of meat, you can find a vegetarian dish: the Tofu Delight is sautéed in olive oil and garlic, and you can choose your level of spiciness. Most sandwiches have a full meal option to be accompanied by a salad, jasmine rice, black beans, and corn on the cob.

You can't go wrong with either location, but the seating is limited at both and all tables are seat yourself. The Fremont location offers a few tables indoors while the Ballard location only offers some outdoor picnic tables off to the side of the unmistakable pink building as seating. The best bet is to pick up your meals and head less than a mile down the road to grab a table at Golden Gardens Park. Oh, and don't forget the napkins!

SPUD $ ♻

2666 Alki Ave. SW, Seattle, WA 98116
(206) 938-0606
MON–SUN 11:00 a.m.–9:00 p.m.
www.facebook.com/AlkiSpud

Located on Alki Avenue, the original Spud is the perfect mix of fish, salt, and fresh air. There are three locations throughout the Seattle area: Greenlake, Juanita (in Kirkland), and the original in West Seattle on Alki. Originally opened in 1935, Spud on Alki is still in the same building as when it was merely a seasonal seaside culinary shack. Today this legendary Seattle staple is two floors and seats eighty-plus people. The top floor (my favorite seating area) has a beautiful view of the boardwalk and the ocean. On my most recent visit, I enjoyed my meal while watching the sunset. You can have the typical (no less delicious) cod fish-and-chips meal, or splurge for halibut, prawns, scallops, oysters, or clams. My personal favorite is the oysters-and-chips meal. The oysters are the perfect combination of crispy breaded outside and a moist, juicy, flavorful inside.

Not to be overlooked, the fries are no side dish to the fish. They are hand-cut (fresh, not frozen) and deep fried in small batches right there in front of you. They also offer milkshakes made with real ice cream. Though the food is amazing, the best part of Spud on Alki is the experience. Though parking can be difficult (to say the least) on a nice sunny day, it's part of the experience to park a few blocks away and enjoy the sunshine on the way over. However, there is a parking lot designated solely for Spud customers that can ease your parking woes.

Spud has both composting and recycling options and utilizes compostable plastic condiment containers. If deep-fried seafood, salty fresh air, and hand-cut fries are on your mind, Spud on Alki is the place to go.

CHEAP EATS

DICK'S DRIVE-IN $
Various locations throughout Seattle
SUN–SAT 10:30 a.m.–2:00 a.m.
www.dicksdrivein.com

Dick's Drive-In is Seattle's oldest continuously operating fast-food restaurant. The menu is simple, the food is cheap, and they're cash only. Their menu consists of four types of burgers, fries, shakes, soda, and ice cream. This iconic burger joint is open until 2:00 a.m. and gets packed around the time bartenders yell, "Last call!"

I like to order a Dick's Deluxe Burger and fries to go and then take them home and douse them in Thousand Island dressing and maybe some caramelized onions. The end result is very close to In-N-Out's animal style burger, and it hits the spot after a night out on the town with friends.

EL CHUPACABRA $ V
6711 Greenwood Ave. N., Seattle, WA 98103
(206) 706-4889
MON–FRI 11:00 a.m.–2:00 a.m.
SAT–SUN 2:00 p.m.–2:00 a.m.
www.myspace.com/chupacabra_bar

If the weather is warm enough for you to seek a nice outdoor deck and a couple of stellar margaritas, then head north for El Chupacabra. The restaurant sits inside a converted house in Phinney Ridge, and the deck overlooks Greenwood at the southernmost corner of the zoo. The food is simple and inexpensive, burritos from $5.50 to $7.95, tacos from $2.50 for one, or taco plates from $4.95 to $6.95 depending on your choice of filling. Plus enchiladas, tostadas, and all the standard Mexican fare, all under $9.95. The nachos are basic but tasty, and the guacamole is always fresh. Vegetarian/vegan-friendly, this place offers fake-steak or faux-chicken at no extra charge, as well as carnivore-friendly carne asada, chicken, and shrimp. The bar is always full, and with a long list of margaritas, there is good reason. The chupacabra theme is apparent everywhere, so if you aren't into mythical alien creatures or loud music from the jukebox, stick to the deck and don't wander too far inside. Either way, you will always get your money's worth at this quirky neighborhood find.

SPLURGE

Chez Shea $$$$ Local
94 Pike St., Ste. 34, Seattle, WA 98101
(206) 467-9990
TUE–SUN 5:00 p.m.–Closing
www.chezshea.com

Perched above Pike Place Market, Chez Shea is a great spot for a romantic dinner featuring fresh, local cuisine. It is the first restaurant my husband and I visited in Seattle and remains one of our favorites. Reservations are recommended as the restaurant is quite small and the best spots in the house—along the window overlooking Pike Place Market—are taken quickly. I also recommend that you come hungry, but not starving, and ready to enjoy the atmosphere and each other's company; true to its French roots, the service is laid back and never rushed.

While we've heard the tasting menus are good, we typically like a more customized meal and always end up ordering from the seasonal menu. Raw oysters are a personal favorite, and I can almost never pass up fresh local ones! I was particularly excited on my most recent visit to Chez Shea when I saw they were featuring Snow Creek Pacific oysters, and so I decided to start our meal with a half dozen. Unlike many oysters you typically find at Seattle restaurants, such as Kusshi and Kumamoto, Snow Creek oysters are larger and richer in flavor. While the Cucumber Namasu and Mango-Pear Mignonette topping was a beautiful complement, note these aren't for the novice oyster eater.

We finished our first course with a fromage plate—it never disappoints! Our favorite was a soft cow's milk cheese from Whidbey Island.

For our second course, we selected the Seared Foie Gras and Pear Salad. If you like foie gras, you need to eat at Chez Shea. Always served on toasted brioche with a sauce made from fresh local fruit, this dish provides that perfect combination of sweet, buttery goodness finished with a crunch. This is one of the better preparations I've had. The pear salad was dressed with a fantastic honey champagne vinaigrette and is a dish I would definitely order again.

Clearly one of Chez Shea's advantages is its proximity to Pike Place Market and the plethora of local ingredients available there. I think one area where Chez Shea excels is preparing those local ingredients in a way that highlights the freshness—the primary reason I chose to have my first sample of this season's Copper River sockeye salmon here.

Available for less than a month, fresh Copper River sockeye salmon is undoubtedly one of the best fish out there and just one more reason living in Seattle is amazing. True to my expectations, Chez Shea served the salmon with fresh veggies and a very simple lime sauce that complemented the fish perfectly. An amazing dish to finish an amazing meal!

DANIEL'S BROILER $$$$

809 Fairview Pl. N., Seattle, WA 98109
(206) 621-8262
SUN–MON 5:00 p.m.–9:00 p.m.
TUE–THU 5:00 p.m.–10:00 p.m.
FRI–SAT 5:00 p.m.–11:00 p.m.
www.schwartzbros.com/daniels.cfm

Once in a while you have to treat yourself, and if you're a carnivore, there's nothing more satisfying than a sizzling steak. Now I must admit that paying seventy-five dollars for a steak is a little hard to swallow, but I just so happened to have seventy-five dollars' worth of gift cards to any Schwartz restaurant of my choosing, so I told my girlfriend I was taking her out to dinner Friday night.

The hostess gave us a brief introduction to the restaurant and showcased the different cuts of USDA prime steaks before escorting us to our table. I ordered the bone-in, medium-rare filet mignon with the béarnaise sauce and seasonal veggies. My girlfriend ordered the halibut with fresh tarragon over a bed of pasta. The steak was superb. It had a hard, crispy shell and was so tender on the inside that I barely had to chew it. I even had a chance to speak with the head chef about how he managed to do this. He told me the trick is to broil the steak first at 1800 degrees, which chars the outside and forms a shell that will retain all of the juices from the meat. They use Lawry's Seasoned Salt to coat the meat, and the sugars in the seasoning form the caramelized shell. From there, all you have to do is cook the steak on the grill until the desired temperature.

The sommelier was knowledgeable and unpretentious. He recommended a local Grenache from McCrae Cellars. This jammy wine with strong strawberry notes and spices was the perfect complement to my steak and even came in a half-bottle option. We mentioned that we were planning a trip to visit Yakima Valley's vineyards, and the sommelier gave us his card and told us to flaunt it shamelessly at every vineyard since they know him well and we would receive a discount.

Normally, the bill for a fine-dining experience such as the one we had at Daniel's would give me a heart attack. However, my gift card, along with platinum membership, which entitled me to another 5 percent discount, was enough to keep my blood pressure down. It will probably be a long time before I set foot inside Daniel's again (need another gift card first!), but if you want to treat yourself and splurge on a good meal and a terrific dining experience, Daniel's is the place to go.

How to Cook a Wolf $$–$$$

2208 Queen Anne Ave. N., Seattle, WA 98109
(206) 838-8090
SUN–THU 5:00 p.m.–11:00 p.m.
FRI–SAT 5:00 p.m.–12:00 a.m.
www.ethanstowellrestaurants.com/howtocookawolf/
Reservations recommended

In M. F. K. Fisher's culinary classic *How to Cook a Wolf*, she challenges her readers to eat and to eat well using simple ingredients, even during a time when the wolf is knocking at the door. Visitors to Ethan Stowell's How to Cook a Wolf on the top of Queen Anne are able to revel in eating simple ingredients prepared well with no regard for the wolf. The restaurant itself is small and intimate with only a single row of tables lined against a wall of thin wood panels that stretch from floor to ceiling and curve at the top to present a modern ski chalet atmosphere. The menu is Italian inspired and changes daily, although staples continually reappear on the menu. Each dish is a small plate easily shared by two with the pastas being slightly larger.

Highlights of the ever-changing menu include escolar crudo prepared with avocado, grapefruit, and chili, or the soft boiled eggs sliced in half, slightly runny, and topped with an anchovy filet and an olive, presenting an amazing bite. On the more substantial side are things such as the chicken liver mousse generously portioned on crostini, or the seared scallops on top of an olive relish with artichokes. If you have saved room, the handmade pastas never disappoint—try the tagliarini prepared in an egg sauce and topped with bacon and onion. The richness of the egg sauce combined with the bacon and onion is delicious and suggestive of eating pasta for breakfast. It is hard to say the pastas steal the show from the dozen or so plates, but they provide a great balance to the meal.

There is also seating at the bar that offers the same menu and the opportunity to watch the chefs prepare the plates with precision. The wine list follows the theme of simple Italian style. All of the staff are well versed in wine selections and can offer tips to pair with the dishes.

Whether the wolf is knocking at the door or you want to celebrate his absence, How to Cook a Wolf provides food and an experience not soon to be forgotten.

Waterfront Seafood Grill $$$$
2801 Alaskan Way, Pier 70, Seattle, WA 98121
(206) 956-9171
SUN–THU 5:00 p.m.–10:00 p.m.
FRI–SAT 5:00 p.m.–11:00 p.m.
www.waterfrontpier70.com

Located at the end of Pier 70 with amazing views of Puget Sound and superior staff, service, and cuisine, Waterfront Seafood Grill is a seafood and fine-dining lover's dream. To take full advantage of the view, reservations with a request to be seated by the window are recommended. Ask to sit outside during the summer months, and don't worry about an evening chill—as soon as you even think you may need a sweater, the waitstaff is at your table with warm, fluffy blankets! Regardless of where you sit, your evening will certainly begin with a warm greeting, reminiscent of Southern hospitality and only the beginning of a fantastic experience.

Home to the Washington Wine Commission's Sommelier of the Year, Kristen Young, the wine list is extensive and created to perfectly complement Executive Chef Peter Levine's creations. Kristen and her staff are always available to help you select a bottle (or glass) that fits your palate and price range. A lover of Willamette Valley wines, we selected the King Estate Pinot Gris 2008, which once again reaffirmed our confidence in the staff to guide us to a wine that suits our tastes. (Hint:

WSG is also a wine retailer, so if you don't finish your bottle, they are happy to package it for you to take home.)

Given that WSG has one of the best views in Seattle, it's a restaurant where you'll want to order several courses. The staff is again always willing to help you select the order in which to enjoy your selections or allow you to tell them exactly how you want them. For our most recent visit, my husband and I started with the steamed Manila clams. Served with roasted fennel and tomatoes and crispy bacon, these clams were fantastic. To take full advantage, make sure you dip your bread in the broth!

Next we moved on to our own version of a second course—spicy crab bisque and seasonal mixed greens. The mixed greens were selected to up the nutritional value of our meal but turned out to be much more than that. They were served with goat cheese, walnuts, and a lemon citronette, and my husband was sure to eat every last bite—a rare occurrence when salad is involved! The spicy crab bisque was undoubtedly the star of this course, however. As someone raised in the South where she-crab soup is a staple, I must say I was skeptical of a "new" type of crab soup, which also features sherry. I should not have been—this bisque was perfectly prepared. Rich and velvety with a flawless combination of sherry, Johnnie Walker Red Label, and fresh Dungeness crab, it is a must-have for future visits.

Deciding which fish to eat for the main course can be daunting at times—they are all beautifully prepared and fresh-frozen at the least. I tend to ask my server what the freshest fish in-house is and go with that; it always serves me well and typically results in new knowledge about the Seattle seafood scene. As a result, we ended our meal (no room for dessert) with the grilled halibut and a side of macaroni and cheese (the extra

$9 to finish the mac 'n' cheese with Dungeness crab is a must in my book). Served with lobster, corn, sweet peas, bacon, and sweet butter, the halibut was very fresh and was a perfect end to a perfect meal. We packaged most of the mac 'n' cheese for lunch the following day—it made great leftovers!

Needless to say, Waterfront Seafood Grill has become one of my favorite restaurants in Seattle and one of my favorite seafood restaurants in general. Considering that I was raised in a seafood restaurant, I see this as no small feat. Well done!

LATE NIGHT

THE HIGHLINE $-$$ V
10 Broadway Ave. E., Seattle, WA 98102
(206) 328-7837
MON–FRI 11:00 a.m.–2:00 a.m.
SAT–SUN 9:00 a.m.–2:00 a.m.
www.highlineseattle.com

Situated above an adult superstore in one of Seattle's most bar-packed neighborhoods, the Highline is a vegan pub in which all late-night eaters, carnivorous or otherwise, will feel instantly at home. The décor is minimal, part greasy spoon, part indie rock club. The floor space is crammed with wobbly two-person tables you can push together or pull apart to accommodate groups of all sizes. There are shelves full of board games and an outdoor deck with seating that overlooks busy Broadway below.

The beer on tap ranges from a $2 PBR served in a pint glass to a $7 Duchesse de Bourgogne in a graceful goblet, with a range of microbrews in between. The Highline also distills some of its own alcohols, including a homemade lavender vodka that is delicious in a martini or mixed with some St. Germain and soda. For those who like a kick after midnight, the garlic and habanero vodka makes a Bloody Mary you won't soon forget. But at the heart of the matter is the food. The entire menu is vegan-friendly, but forget your preconceived ideas about what that means. At the Highline, there are no small portions or fancy, frilly vegetable concoctions. Their poutine puts dairy-based versions of the same dish to shame: crispy french fries smothered in mounds of salty brown gravy and vegan cottage cheese. The sandwiches include an array of veggie burgers, a "fish" burger with or without "cheez," "chicken" tenders on an oversized roll, and a BBQ "pork" slider, just to name a few. My personal favorite is the smoky Rueben on marbled rye, heaped high with sauerkraut and all the trimmings. It's around $7 for sandwiches alone, $10 for a sandwich plus your choice of a side: coleslaw, potato salad, or a small plate of mixed greens. There are also apps, wraps, and even some larger main courses if your late-night appetite demands something more along the lines of mushroom pasta or fake-steak and potatoes. If you're up before 2:00 p.m. on the weekends, stop back in for brunch. Night or day, you won't be disappointed here.

Il Bistro $$$$

93-A Pike St., Seattle, WA 98101
(206) 682-3049
SUN–SAT 5:30 p.m.–10:00 p.m.
SUN–THU 10:00 p.m.–12:00 a.m. (late-night menu)
FRI–SAT 11:00 p.m.–1:00 a.m. (late-night menu)
www.ilbistro.net

Tucked just below Pike Place Market, Il Bistro is a perfect spot for a romantic late-night bite or dessert. Seating is available at the bar, where the selection of grappas is beautifully displayed and the bartenders show off their expert preparation of martinis, or at any of the intimate, candlelit bar tables. Both seating areas are great, so if the crowd hasn't decided for you, I recommend choosing based on your mood and company.

On our most recent visit we were in the mood for something sweet accompanied by a nice port, so, with the help of our server, we selected the Warre's Otima 10-Year Tawny Port, tiramisu, and chocolate torte. The port was exactly what we requested—smooth and not too sweet. The torte was well prepared and served with fresh cream and a raspberry coulis, both very nice complements to the richness of the torte. The star of our dessert was certainly the tiramisu, however. It had all the right elements, down to the entire plate—not just the cake—receiving a generous dusting of cocoa powder.

Il Bistro is definitely a spot we'll continue to stop in on late nights and is one we've added to our "must try for dinner" list!

Pie $ V

3515 Fremont Ave. N., Seattle, WA 98103
(206) 436-8590
TUES–SAT 10:00 a.m.–8:00 p.m.
SUN 10:00 a.m.–6:00 p.m.
Late-night window FRI–SAT 9:00 p.m.–2:00 a.m.
www.sweetandsavorypie.com

America hasn't quite caught on to the concept of savory pies, but one shop—appropriately named Pie—is breaking the mold. Located just north of the Fremont Bridge, Pie offers a variety of sweet and savory pies. However, since most people in this country think of pie as a sweet dish, I'm going to focus on the savory pies.

Their savory selection includes a roasted red bell pepper and potato pie, a pesto veggie pie, a decadent mac 'n' cheese pie, a peppered bacon and egg scramble pie, and, my personal favorite, an English meat pie. These pies look small but are surprisingly filling. I stumbled upon their late-night pickup window (open until 2:00 a.m.!) while walking home one night and ordered the English meat pie. It was so good that I wolfed it down even though it singed the roof of my mouth! Word on the street is that they'll soon be offering a BBQ pork pie, too!

WEST MEETS EAST

Annapurna Café $$–$$$ V
1833 Broadway, Seattle, WA 98122
(206) 320-7770
MON–THU 12:00 p.m.–9:30 p.m.
FRI–SAT 12:00 p.m.–10:00 p.m.
SUN 4:00 p.m.–9:00 p.m.
www.annapurnacafe.com

The name Annapurna refers to series of peaks in the Himalayas. Living up to its name, Annapurna Café offers unique eating choices from the region of Nepal, Tibet, and India, including several vegetarian and vegan delicacies. Meals start with delicious appetizers such as the Tibetan specialty vegetarian spinach momo, the vegetarian Nepalese preparation called aloo dum, and popular Indian appetizers such as samosas and pakoras. Annapurna's spinach dip is quite unique as it includes the savory fried Indian naan bread with a baked dipping curry made of spinach and Indian cream cheese—paneer.

Main course offerings include unique entrees from the Himalayan regions. The vegan Lhasa curry is a Tibetan-style curry cooked with Tibetan herbs in a creamy tomato sauce. Similarly, you can also enjoy a vegan Nepalese Annapurna curry made with Nepali herbs, and several other options from the Indian subcontinent. The menu does offer several carnivorous selections prepared with Nepalese, Tibetan, and Indian herbs and recipes.

Among many unique cocktails and alcohol from the region, Annapurna has some amazing martinis made from saffron-infused vodka. You can also enjoy the Yeti, Lhasa, or Tikka Gold beers from the Himalayan region.

Finding parking near Annapurna is quite a task but is also a common challenge with all the business establishments in the Capitol Hill area. The restaurant's decor features pictures of the Himalayan summits and tourists enjoying the local culture and places. From the ceiling hang several Buddhist prayer flags, which are inscribed with auspicious symbols, invocations, prayers, and mantras that are commonplace in the Buddhist houses of the region.

Annapurna Café is an ideal place to experience the meals of a Sherpa within Seattle.

ARAYA'S PLACE $$-$$$ **V**

1121 NE 45th St., Seattle, WA 98105

(206) 524-4332

MON–THU 11:30 a.m.–9:30 p.m.

FRI–SAT 11:30 a.m.–10:00 p.m.

SUN 11:30 a.m.–3:30 p.m.

www.arayasplace.com

Araya's offers a unique vegan Thai experience. Thai cuisine is known to use fish water and fish sauce as a base, but you will find none of that at Araya's, which makes this place a special treat for hard-core vegans and vegetarians. Araya's also offers veggie substitute meats for the carnivorous palates.

You can start your meal by indulging with the tom yum or tom kah soups. All soups are served family style (serving four). The tom yum soup is my personal favorite as it is a delicately flavored, healthy soup that helps clear your throat and sinuses. For appetizers try the veggie satay, various vegetables served on a skewer and accompanied by a peanut sauce.

Main course favorites include the kaeng ka-ri and pa-nang curry. Kaeng ka-ri is a sumptuous Thai yellow curry that includes the seldom-used (in Thai cuisine) potato. Pa-nang curry traces the Malaysian influence on Thai cuisine and is considered milder than the other Thai curries. You can order brown or jasmine rice to go along with the main course. The menu also offers a good selection of Thai noodles.

At Araya's you can also enjoy a broad selection of Asian teas, such as the delicately flavored jasmine blossom tea, as well as the more exotic in-shell coconut juice or cactus juice.

Araya's ambience shows a distinct Thai influence. You are treated with Buddhist deity statues from the moment you enter.

You can see the symbolic food offering to the deities, a Thai cultural tradition. During peak dinner hours, the parking scene at the restaurant can often get tricky.

CEDARS $$–$$$ V
4759 Brooklyn Ave. NE, Seattle, WA 98105
(206) 527-4000
MON–SAT 11:30 a.m.–10:00 p.m.
SUN 11:00 a.m.–9:30 p.m.
www.cedarsseattle.com

Cedars Restaurant is an Indian restaurant serving cuisine from northern India as well as kabobs and Mediterranean platters. Cedars Restaurant offers some of the best Indian naan bread (plain or flavored), served with dipping sauce or any of the curries. The Indian curries are cooked in authentic Indian home style with flavorful herbs. Spice levels can be adjusted as per the individual palate preferences. My personal favorites include the vegan okra masala and the vegetarian dal (lentil) maharani.

Cedars Restaurant also highlights some of the best beer selections from around the globe, including popular Indian beers such as Kingfisher, Taj Mahal, and Haywards. You can choose from the bottled beer options in refrigerators near the entrance, or try a nonalcoholic, yogurt-based Indian drink called lassi (plain or flavored) or an unlimited serving of Indian tea—chai—one of the favorites of the Cedars Restaurant patrons.

An old University District house that has been repurposed into a restaurant, Cedars Restaurant has a unique ambience. During the summer, the restaurant also offers outdoor seating.

Cedars has very limited reserved parking spots in the Safeway grocery parking lot. Your safest bet is to find street parking near the restaurant.

HONORABLE MENTIONS

PICK-QUICK $ 🏷️Local ♻️
1132 Auburn Way N., Auburn, WA 98002
(253) 248-1949
MON–SUN 10:30 a.m.–10:00 p.m.
www.pick-quick.com

If you enjoy hand-cut fries, burgers made from grass-fed organic beef, and shakes made with real ice cream, Pick-Quick in Auburn is the place to indulge in your fantasies. Originally opened in Fife over sixty years ago, Pick-Quick is a staple in the South End for burgers and fries. The new Pick-Quick in Auburn is a partnership with the original, but not an exact replica—it has a commitment to keeping the charm and integrity of the original while incorporating modern additions to both the food and design.

I recommend a deluxe burger with fries and a chocolate peanut butter milkshake. The burger is made fresh to order, so it is a winning combination of hot meat and cool, crisp toppings. The fries are hand-cut with the perfect amount of grease and salt. The milkshakes are made with real ice cream from Snoqualmie creamery. The food is amazing, but what I like best about this restaurant is their commitment to being eco-friendly. The tagline prominently displayed below their menu says it all: "Local*Natural*Sustainable: Caring for each other, caring for the earth, one meal at a time." It seems this restaurant has made every effort to be "green," down to the pervious concrete outside allowing water to be recycled and the water-saving toilets. Take an adventure on a sunny Saturday and enjoy your meal out in the sun on one of the many benches. Auburn may seem like a trek for a burger and fries, but I guarantee you won't be disappointed.

PLUM BISTRO $$–$$$ ▨ ♺ V
1429 12th Ave., Seattle, WA 98122
(206) 838-5333
MON–FRI 9:00 a.m.–10:30 p.m.
SAT–SUN 10:00 a.m.–10:30 p.m.
www.plumbistroseattle.com

Plum Bistro is one of Seattle's only all-vegan restaurants serving up three meals a day, seven days a week. Nestled into the southern slope of Capitol Hill, this bright little bistro is well worth the time it takes for your order to arrive at your table. Whether you are looking for a delicious breakfast, both savory and sweet, or a sandwich for lunch, or spicy mac 'n' yease (yeasty vegan "cheese") for dinner, this place has it all.

The tables are small and close together, but the entire front wall of the restaurant is open to the street, which makes the space feel open rather than cramped. The food is made with local, organic ingredients, and is prepared with love—which means that it does take time. I have waited as long as an hour for brunch after placing my order, but the coffee is divine, the cocktails are phenomenal, and the food is so delicious that I have never minded the wait. The breakfast/brunch menus are varied, from the tantalizingly complex Mayan blue corn pancakes served with a jalapeno tofu scramble ($13), to the ultra-sweet strawberry crepes served with a creamy vanilla custard sauce and fresh strawberries ($9), and everything in between—spicy chocolate waffles anyone? ($10)—the menu is sure to please a discerning palate.

Weekday afternoons there is no brunch, but the wraps ($10–11), po'boys ($8), pizzas ($10), and salads ($8–9) are just the tip of the mouthwatering iceberg that carves out the lunch menu. Dinner serves up burgers of all configurations, but my personal favorite is the Crazy Jamaican ($14), jerk tofu patties with ripe plantains, grilled sweet onions, and a mildly spicy sauce that ties it all together. All burgers come with fries (regular or yam), but there is much more than just burgers to choose from: orange balsamic glazed tempeh ($18), country-fried seitan steak ($17), and raw tacos ($13), which are small but super yummy and surprisingly filling.

The cocktails at Plum are chock-full of interesting flavor combinations and tons of fresh ingredients: fruit, herbs, olives, and more. When it's hot out, the Oh My Sweet Goddess ($10) is blissful, strawberry lemonade, vodka, muddled strawberries, lemons, fresh basil, and a splash of agave nectar. No matter what time of day you stop in, make sure you aren't in a hurry, and take the time to savor your meal.

LOCAL WINE AND BEER

BREWERIES AND BEER

REDHOOK BREWERY

14300 NE 145th St., Woodinville, WA 98072

(425) 483-3232

MON–THU 11:00 a.m.–11:00 p.m.

FRI–SAT 11:00 a.m.–12:00 a.m.

SUN 11:00 a.m.–9:00 p.m.

www.redhook.com

Seattle has one of the highest consumption rates of beer per capita of any American city, and the local taste for beer has spurred a robust microbrewing industry with some of the best beers you can find in the country. Redhook Brewery, located in Woodinville, Washington, is a local brewery that began its operations in Seattle in 1981 but has since gone mainstream with national distribution. The brewery operations in Woodinville craft beers and ales of varying types, incorporating local taste preferences.

Regular and seasonal brews include the flagship Redhook ESB (original), Long Hammer (IPA), Redhook Blonde (golden ale), Rope Swing (summer pilsner), Big Ballard (IPA), Copper Hook (copper ale), Mudslinger (nut brown ale), Winter Hook (winter ale), and Late Harvest (autumn ale). My personal favorite is the Mudslinger, a dark nut brown ale brewed in traditional American brown ale brewing style with 5.8% alcohol content and, according to Redhook, best paired with grilled meats, fowl, stews, and smoked oysters or salmon.

Located within the brewery is the Forecaster's Pub, just a few meters from the popular Burke Gilman bike trail. The pub is a great place for bicyclists and Redhook fans to sample various ale offerings and some great pub food. There is plenty of outdoor seating, and I have spent quite a few summer days having a good time soaking in the sun and enjoying great beverages.

The brewery is also a stone's throw away from popular Washington wineries Chateau Ste. Michelle and Columbia, where wine lovers may immerse themselves in tastings of some the best wine Washington has to offer.

If you are new to Seattle or haven't made it to the brewery yet, I highly recommend an outing to Redhook on a bicycle while enjoying the beautiful Burke Gilman trail, which begins in the city and runs around Lake Washington.

LINDA'S TAVERN

707 E. Pine St., Seattle, WA 98122-2234
(206) 325-1220
MON–SUN 4:00 p.m.–2:00 a.m.
www.lindastavern.com

Linda's Tavern, located in the famous Pike-Pine corridor of Seattle's Capitol Hill neighborhood, is a Montana-styled dive bar frequented by an eclectic crowd of students, artists, intellectuals, and professionals alike. The tavern offers a selection of local microbrews at affordable prices with great music and service to top it off. I prefer to get a Maritime Flagship Red Alt Ale, a smooth and well-balanced nutty red amber brewed by the Maritime Pacific Brewery. Expect to find some other local Northwest favorites such as Manny's Pale Ale and Boundary Bay Ale.

Linda's also has my favorite happy hour specials on sliders, nachos, and other bar food from 7:00 p.m. to 9:00 p.m. on weekdays, and it does get busy during those hours. The outdoor patio with a separate bar is a great place to enjoy a sunny summer evening while sampling local microbrews at affordable prices.

The proprietor of the tavern also operates some other successful bars, including King's Hardware in Ballard and Smith on Fifteenth Avenue in Capitol Hill.

FREMONT BREWING COMPANY—URBAN BEER GARDEN

3409 Woodland Park Ave. N., Seattle, WA 98103
Retail Hours:
MON–WED 11:00 a.m.–5:00 p.m.
THURS–FRI 11:00 a.m.–8:00 p.m.
SAT 12:00 p.m.–8:00 p.m.
SUN 12:00 p.m.–5:00 p.m.
Urban Beer Garden Hours:
THURS–FRI 4:00 p.m.–8:30 p.m.
SAT 12:00 p.m.–8:30 p.m.
SUN 12:00 p.m.–5:00 p.m.
www.fremontbrewing.com

Make no mistake: the Fremont Brewing Company is all about beer. You won't find a long food menu. You won't find outward displays of interior decorating. You will find delicious, brewed-on-site craft beer. In the Urban Beer Garden you'll find a few tables and benches made from the old bleachers at Ballard High School, metal bowls full of free pretzels, and beer.

The Universale Pale Ale is their flagship product, and it's a balanced offering. It's a brilliant session beer that will prove agreeable for those in your party who might be wary of strongly hopped Northwest ales. Hops lovers will enjoy the Interurban India Pale Ale, with a fragrant, spicy flavor to please the palate.

Lines can get long on Fridays, which might prompt the management to change things up. That might just mean adding another register, but just in case wholesale changes are in order, you should visit now so you can say you remember when.

The brewery is located in a blue cinderblock warehouse in Fremont, near the intersection of North Thirty-fifth Street and Stone Way, just off of the Burke Gilman trail.

WINE BARS

With the growth of the Washington wine industry, it was only a matter of time before Seattle started seeing wine bars popping up all over. Over the past five years, the Seattle area has seen more of these amazing little establishments crop up. They are not only good options to enjoy wine, but they're often great dining establishments as well. Here we've highlighted some of the more noteworthy.

SIP

Sip (Seattle)
909 Fifth Ave., Seattle, WA 98104
Lunch: MON–FRI 11:30 a.m.–2:00 p.m.
Dinner: MON–SAT 4:30 p.m.–Closing
www.siprestaurant.com

and

Sip (Issaquah)
1084 NE Park Dr., Issaquah, WA 98029
MON–TUES 5:00 p.m.–Closing (seasonal)
WED–FRI 5:00 p.m.–12:00 a.m.
SAT 4:00 p.m.–12:00 a.m.
SUN 4:00 p.m.–Closing (seasonal)

With two locations, Seattle and Issaquah, Sip offers not only a wonderful selection of wines but also a creative menu tailored to complement wine. This upscale restaurant's menu is segmented by lunch, dinner, or small plates and also boasts some amazing desserts that are sure to delight. Sip's global wine menu encompasses over 250 wines from all over the world, but also showcases many of the Northwest's favorites.

PURPLE CAFÉ AND WINE BAR

Purple Café and Wine Bar (Bellevue)
430 106th Ave. NE, Bellevue, WA 98004
(425) 502-6292
MON–THURS 11:00 a.m.–10:00 p.m.
FRI 11:00 a.m.–11:00 p.m.

SAT 12:00 p.m.–11:00 p.m.
SUN 12:00 p.m.–9:00 p.m.
www.thepurplecafe.com

and

Purple Café and Wine Bar (Kirkland)
323 Park Place Center, Kirkland, WA 98033
(425) 828-3772
MON–THURS 11:00 a.m.–10:00 p.m.
FRI–SAT 11:00 a.m.–11:00 p.m.
SUN 11:00 a.m.–9:00 p.m.

and

Purple Café and Wine Bar (Seattle)
1225 Fourth Ave., Seattle, WA 98101
(206) 829-2280
MON–THURS 11:00 a.m.–11:00 p.m.
FRI 11:00 a.m.–12:00 a.m.
SAT 12:00 p.m.–12:00 a.m.
SUN 12:00 p.m.– 11:00 p.m.

and

Purple Café and Wine Bar (Woodinville)
14459 Woodinville Redmond Rd. NE, Woodinville, WA
98072
(425) 483-7129
SUN–THURS 11:00 a.m.–9:00 p.m.
FRI–SAT 11:00 a.m.–10:00 p.m.

With four locations, Purple is always a great choice when looking to enjoy some amazing wine. They showcase a global wine selection and offer customers the option to sample different varieties with a broad "flight" selection. The restaurant also pairs featured wines with varied menu options. They specialize in fresh, seasonal ingredients, and the menu ranges from small plates and salads to pizzas, cheeses, or entrees, depending on your level of hunger. They also offer group-dining options for parties or special events. This mid-scale restaurant's atmosphere can be described as an urban retreat with rustic elements.

THE LOCAL VINE

1410 12th Ave., Seattle, WA 98122
(206) 257-5653
Bottle Shop:
MON–THURS 4:00 p.m.–Closing
FRI–SUN 1:00 p.m.–Closing
Wine Bar:
DAILY 4:00 p.m.–Closing
www.thelocalvine.com

The Local Vine takes a slightly different approach to wine and offers a comfortable and relaxing atmosphere. Offering small plates, they specialize in seasonal, local, organic food that supports the local economy. The Local Vine offers over one hundred wines by the glass, wine tasting classes with a sommelier, and also food events that boast multi-course meals with select wines to complement each dish. As if that wasn't enough, the Local Vine also offers a wine club and retail store to enable customers to continue to enjoy a special varietal at home.

WINERIES AND TASTING ROOMS

Woodinville, WA

Just a short drive northeast from Seattle lies the town of Woodinville, known for its wineries and tasting rooms. The two biggest names are **Chateau Ste. Michelle** and **Columbia Winery**, which offer large grounds to explore and tasting rooms to try the latest releases.

And just up the road, wine enthusiasts can find a collection of tasting rooms including **Novelty Hill Winery** (open daily from 11:00 a.m. to 5:00 p.m.) and **Kestral Vintners** (open Thursday through Monday from 12:00 p.m. to 5:00 p.m., or by appointment), showcasing fantastic Washington wines from delicate Chardonnays to robust Merlots.

One of my favorites is the **Alexandria Nicole Cellars** tasting room, located in the old Hollywood Schoolhouse, a historical landmark originally built in 1912 and renovated in 1994. Alexandria Nicole recently won "Winery of the Year" from *Wine Press Northwest* and was also voted "Best Wine Club." Wines available for tasting include Viognier, Rosé, Sauvignon Blanc, Cabernet Sauvignon, and Syrah. If you choose to join the award-winning wine club, you get access to the "Hidden Door" room where members taste "members-only" releases and receive a 10 percent discount on each bottle purchased.

The Alexandria Nicole Cellars tasting room is open Thursday through Monday from 12:00 p.m. to 5:00 p.m. and offers tapas on the weekends.

Chateau Ste. Michelle is open daily from 10:00 a.m. to 5:00 p.m., with guided tours available from 10:30 a.m. to 4:30 p.m.

The Columbia Winery tasting room is open Sunday through Tuesday from 11:00 a.m. to 6:00 p.m. and Wednesday through Saturday from 11:00 a.m. to 7:00 p.m.

The Tasting Room, Seattle

If you don't have time to head up to Woodinville, the Tasting Room near Pike Place Market is a great place to taste a variety of Washington wines in one place. As a cooperative wine cellar, you can taste wine from Camaraderie Cellars, Harlequin Wine Cellars, Latitude 46 N, Mountain Dome Winery, NHV Winery, Wilridge Winery, and Wineglass Cellars.

The Tasting Room's hours are Sunday through Thursday from 12:00 p.m. to 8:00 p.m. and Friday and Saturday from 12:00 p.m. to late.

FARMERS MARKETS

There is a fantastic variety of farmers markets in the Seattle area for shopping, snacking, and people-watching. Although we call them "farmers" markets, many artisans also participate and offer their original works for sale. Most neighborhood markets operate on only one day of the week,  so knowing the schedule and planning ahead will prevent disappointment. Some vendors travel from market to market; for example, if you bought a tasty turnip from a farmer in Edmonds on Saturday, with a little research you can find his market stall in Lake Forest Park on Sunday and buy a few pounds more.

Here's a list of markets, their days of operation, and their locations as of May 2011.

Seattle:

- **Cascade** (South Lake Union, Wednesdays, 3:00 p.m.–7:00 p.m.), Minor Ave. between Thomas & Harrison St.
- **Broadway** (Sundays, 11:00 a.m.–3:00 p.m., May–December), Broadway & Pine at Seattle Central Community College on Capitol Hill, 98102, http://www.seattlefarmersmarkets.org/markets/broadway
- **Columbia City** (Wednesdays, 3:00 p.m.–7:00 p.m., April–October), 37th Ave. S. & S. Edmunds St., South Seattle, 98118, http://www.seattlefarmersmarkets.org/markets/columbia_city
- **Lake City** (Thursdays, 3:00 p.m.–7:00 p.m., June–October), NE 125th & 28th NE, next to the library off Lake City Way, 98125, http://www.seattlefarmersmarkets.org/markets/lake_city
- **Magnolia** (Saturdays, 10:00 a.m.–2:00 p.m., June–October), 33rd Ave. W. & W. Smith St. in the Magnolia Village, http://www.seattlefarmersmarkets.org/markets/magnolia
- **Phinney** (Fridays, 3:00 p.m.–7:00 p.m., June–October), 67th & Phinney Ave. N., in lower lot of the Phinney Neighborhood Ctr., 98103, http://www.seattlefarmersmarkets.org/markets/phinney
- **University District** (Saturdays, 9:00 a.m.–2:00 p.m., year-round), corner of 50th and University Way NE, in the University Heights lot, 98105, http://www.seattlefarmersmarkets.org/markets/u_district

- **West Seattle** (Sundays, 10:00 a.m.–2:00 p.m., year-round), California Ave. SW & SW Alaska, in the heart of the West Seattle Junction, 98116, http://www. seattlefarmersmarkets.org/markets/west_seattle

North End:
- **Edmonds** (Saturdays, 10:00 a.m.–2:00 p.m., May–October), 5th and Bell St., http://snohomishmarkets com/#Edmonds
- **Lake Forest Park** (Sundays, 10:00 a.m.–2:00 p.m., May–October), Bothell Way and Lake City Way, http:// www.thirdplacecommons.org/farmersmarket/
- **Everett** (Sundays, 11:00 a.m.–4:00 p.m., June–October), West Marine View Dr. (in the Everett Marina parking lot), http://www.everettfarmersmarket.com/

Since it's impossible to cover every farmers market in the greater Seattle area, we've decided to share our absolute favorites here. All these markets are on the list above, and remember, this list is not comprehensive. A bit of research in your own neighborhood could very well uncover a new or established market we haven't captured here.

OUR FAVORITE FARMERS MARKETS

Disclaimer: Farmers markets are dynamic events with vendors that change on a weekly basis. The following reflects the markets on the day(s) we visited them; we can't guarantee that any of the vendors we mention in this chapter will be at the markets when you visit them, too. And that's the fun of it!

Favorite Market for Vegetables
Edmonds Farmers Market
The Edmonds market attracts both the "local" farmers from the Kent Valley and the farmers from the Yakima Valley east of

the Cascades. This variety gives shoppers the best of both climates and a wide selection of vegetables. The warmer climate of Yakima produces yummy asparagus and tasty potatoes in early May, while the Kent Valley will produce tender lettuce and every squash you can name (and some you can't) well into October. The farmers are willing to answer your questions about their produce, what's ripening back on the farm, and what will be ready for market next week. If you're interested in organic vegetables, there are some farmers that advertise "organic vegetables" on signs in their stalls. There are also farmers who are working towards their organic certification, and they will answer your questions about their pest management and fertilizing practices.

Favorite Market for Cheese
University District Farmers Market
Of course, nothing can compare to the variety of cheeses at Pike Place Market (see the chapter on Major Attractions). However,

if you're looking for a great variety in a more low-key environment, the U District's farmers market, held on Saturdays, is a great place to find local cheese of all milks and flavors. Held in a church parking lot (and spilling over in the summer months and during the yearly U District Street Fair), the market is easy to access by bus or by car.

When we went, there were booths with goat, sheep, and cow's milk cheeses. The friendly cheesemakers give out samples of all their cheeses; favorites were a goat's milk blue cheese and cow's milk garlic and dill cheese curds (though this "squeaky cheese" comes in all flavors). The cheese stands tend to be along the front entrance, conveniently located next to some bakers, including an organic bakery. If you like cheese but are shopping for other things, too, hit the cheese stands last—otherwise you risk spending all your money right there!

Favorite Market for Street Food and for Produce
Ballard Farmers Market

The Ballard farmers market is our favorite place to be when you're hungry for lunch on a sunny Sunday and want to enjoy some delicious street food. This market entices its visitors with yummy wood-fired pizza, comforting hot dogs, and European crepes. If you have a hard time resisting all these delicious offers and need a little digestion break after all the indulging, sit down in one of the street cafés—the Ballard farmers market is also a great spot for people- and dog-watching.

This market also shines with a huge variety of fresh produce right in the city. We stock up on produce to get our vitamins back in balance after the street food we just indulged in. Local farms like Full Circle, an organic farm that also delivers produce boxes to residents' doorsteps, sell their delicious seasonal produce. Just a glance proves to you that these veggies, fruits, and herbs were still in the soil (or on the tree) not too long ago. During this stroll we never forget to take home a bottle of the Rockridge Orchard apple cider.

Favorite "Yard Sale" Market
Fremont Sunday Market

The Fremont Sunday Market is far more than "just" a farmers market. This year-round market attracts droves of people not just for the homemade jams and street food, but also for the extensive crafts, antiques, and flea market booths. You can get everything from bracelet bongs to used shoes to fine silver and china. Booths line the streets, some for crafts and some for items you're more likely to find at a yard sale, but the flea market itself is in a cool underground parking structure, protected from both the rain and the sun. This is an excellent place for treasure hunts of all sorts, whether you're looking for Beanie Babies, hand-painted dishes from Poland, new rags, or old records. It would be easy to spend hours pawing through the stands, tables, booths, and racks, so make sure you have time in abundance when attending this market!

Favorite Market for Meat
West Seattle Farmers Market

This farmers market is held on Sundays and offers a great selection of natural, free-range, and organic meats. We like to shop here for big summer barbeques because we can get it all: chicken, beef, turkey, pork... And if you're not sure what your guests will like or what cut of meat is best for the barbeque, the friendly vendors will be more than happy to help out with tips and tricks.

Favorite Farmers Market Special Event
Everett Farmers Market and "Fresh Paint"

Once a year, the Everett farmers market combines with an arts festival called Fresh Paint. The farmers market is always picturesque, on the Everett Marina with the Cascades in the background (and plenty of parking), but Fresh Paint adds an extra dimension. Extending from the market in the parking lot next to Lombardi's Italian restaurant all the way down the boardwalk to Anthony's Homeport, more than a hundred crafters, photographers, and artists come out. Those amazing photographers who haunt Leavenworth's park? Check. Oil painters creating landscapes before our very eyes? Check. Face painters for the kids? Check. Sculptures for the garden? Check. Hand-crafted jewelry of all sorts? Check.

This festival is worth the forty-five-minute trip up I-5, especially on a sunny day. Expect crowds, enjoy the scenery, and support local artists and farmers.

Favorite Farmers Market Location
The Farm Boat at South Lake Union

Climb onboard the *Virginia V*, a wooden steamboat built in 1922 and registered as a National Historic Landmark Vessel. The ship once chartered passengers on Seattle–Bainbridge and Seattle–Tacoma routes, but now it offers up one of Puget Sound's most unique settings for a farmers market. The market offers up everything from handmade chocolate truffles to freshly picked greens, and while you shop you can explore all three levels of the former Mosquito Fleet ship from stem to stern, admiring the pristine engine and peeking into the wheel room. Tables on the aft deck let you enjoy your goodies right on the spot, with prime views for watching the float planes land

and take off or the sailing lessons at the Center for Wooden Boats. And being firmly attached to the dock means a minimal amount of movement, so sea legs aren't required even for our landlubber friends. Mind the gap, though; the step between dock and ship does widen with the water's movement.

ARTS

Seattle has a great appreciation for art, and it is showcased throughout the city. What most people don't know is that Seattle was one of the first cities in the United States that adopted a percent-for-art ordinance, which happened in 1973. The ordinance states that the city will accept responsibility for expanding the public experience with visual art. This ordinance has impacted Seattle's view on art, not only from a public standpoint, but it has also extended into other mediums as well. Being known for rain has some benefits. Seattleites kept inside have prompted some creativity that is evident all throughout the city in different forms.

CLASSICAL MUSIC IN SEATTLE

All classical music lovers who live in Seattle are blessed. The city, along with its suburbs, offers a rich selection of classical music venues. The list includes Bellevue Philharmonic, Bellingham Festival of Music, Seattle Chamber Music Society Summer Festival, Early Music Guild of Seattle, Northwest Symphony Orchestra, Olympic Music Festival, Orchestra Seattle and the Seattle Chamber Singers, Sammamish Symphony Orchestra, Seattle Chamber Music Festival, Seattle Festival Orchestra, Seattle Opera, Seattle Philharmonic Orchestra, and Seattle Symphony.

EARLY MUSIC GUILD (EMG) AND SEATTLE BAROQUE ORCHESTRA

Town Hall Seattle
1119 Eighth Ave., Seattle, WA 98101
(206) 325-7066
www.earlymusicguild.org

EMG consists of a well-selected repertoire of music from the Middle Ages. EMG's mission is "to advance our community's appreciation for music from the Middle Ages through the eighteenth century by providing performances, support, and education." The newly expanded concert season of twelve programs includes baroque music and opera among many early music masterpieces.

NORTHWEST SYMPHONY ORCHESTRA (NWSO)

Highline Performing Arts Center
401 S. 152nd St., Burien, WA 98148
(206) 242-6321
www.northwestsymphonyorchestra.org

Founded in 1987, NWSO's mission is "to be the premier orchestra in the performance and promotion of music by contemporary Northwest composers while also performing, promoting, and educating the public about the full spectrum of classical music." To date, NWSO's focus is twofold: a) to advance the cause of contemporary composers in the Northwest, and b) to perform historical classics. Recently, the NWSO reached the milestone of performing one hundred works by local Northwest composers.

OLYMPIC MUSIC FESTIVAL

Olympic Music Festival Barn
7360 Center Rd., Quilcene, WA 98376
(360) 732-4800
www.olympicmusicfestival.org

Since 1984, the Olympic Music Festival has been enriching the lives of Seattleites by offering a wide selection of chamber and popular classical music. The festival runs from June to early September. The venue is outdoors and suitable for bringing a picnic lunch and enjoying Seattle's spectacular summer afternoons outside. Performances are broadcast locally on Seattle's classical music station 98.1 KING-FM and nationally on 88.5 KPLU, National Public Radio's "Performance Today."

SEATTLE SYMPHONY ORCHESTRA

200 University St., Seattle, WA 98101
(206) 215-4747
www.seattlesymphony.org

Under the new direction of conductor Ludovic Morlot, the Seattle Symphony offers a rich program with extensive variety that promises to satisfy the musical appetite of all patrons. The program starts in September and features world-renowned visiting artists and orchestras as well as special concerts designed just for families. In 1998, the Seattle Symphony Orchestra moved to its beautiful new home, Benaroya Hall, a must visit for all new or veteran lovers of classical music. If you have children, a great place to visit is Soundbridge, where children of all ages come to explore symphonic music through exhibits, classes, and live music presentations.

SEATTLE OPERA

Marion Oliver McCaw Hall
321 Mercer St., Seattle, WA 98109
(800) 426-1619
www.seattleopera.org

The Seattle Opera boasts the highest per-capita attendance of the major opera companies in the United States through its main stage performances. The Seattle Opera also serves thousands more through community and outreach programs. The Seattle Opera is recognized as the United States' premiere presenter of Wagner operas. The Seattle Opera performs five operas per year. The performances are held in beautiful McCaw Hall.

THE VISUAL ARTS SCENE

Seattle's dedication to visual art is showcased throughout the city. In almost any location you can uncover a gallery or structure that represents that area's personality. We'll explore a few of Seattle's neighborhoods and unique visual icons that give each area its own feel.

Fremont

Fremont is probably best known for its visual art that showcases the eccentricity of Fremont, which is also locally known as "the Center of the Universe." If you're in the neighborhood, it might be worth your while to check out the following sites.

The Statue of Lenin
Location: On the corner of N. 36th St., Fremont Pl., and Evanston Ave. N.

The statue was brought to Fremont from Slovakia by a local art lover. After communism was overthrown, Lewis Carpenter (a local bronze artist) bought the statue for $13,000 and had it shipped to his home in Issaquah. After an accident that took his life, the family was left to find it a home. They contacted Peter Bevis, who helped the family move the statue to Fremont.

The Fremont Rocket
Location: Between N. Evanston Ave. and N. Fremont Ave.

The rocket was constructed in the 1950s and was previously affixed to an army surplus store in Belltown. When the store went out of business, the Fremont Business Association snapped up the rocket and brought it to its new home. After a little TLC, a new nose, and some fins, the rocket was ready for the public. The rocket bears the Fremont crest and motto, "De Libertas Quirkas," which means "Freedom to be Peculiar." Beneath the rocket you'll find a coin box affixed to the building. Drop in fifty cents and the rocket will "launch" by blowing a bunch of steam, but unfortunately this rocket will never make it to orbit.

Waiting for the Interurban
Location: N. 34th St. and Fremont Ave. N.

This sculpture was created in 1979, is based out of cast aluminum, and is one of Seattle's most decorated landmarks.

It commemorates the light rail Interurban line that used to connect downtown Seattle with all of its neighborhoods. The statue frequently hosts costumes and "art attacks," and is used to celebrate just about anything. The only rule to play is no commercial messages, clean up after you're finished, and have fun!

The Fremont Troll

Location: N. 36th St. at Troll Ave. N., under the north end of the Aurora Bridge

The Fremont Troll, aka the *Troll Under the Bridge,* is exactly what it sounds like! Built in 1990, the concrete troll stands at nearly twenty feet tall and weighs in at thirteen thousand pounds. The troll was built by four Seattle artists: Steve Badanes, Will Martin, Donna Walter, and Ross Whitehead. It was created with the intention of rehabilitating the property under the bridge because it was being used as a dumping ground and a haven for drug dealers.

Now the troll looks down on you with its one good eye (a hubcap, apparently) and crushes a Volkswagen Beetle with its left hand. When visiting the troll, you are encouraged to climb on it, try to poke his hubcap eye out, and stick your hand inside his oversized nose. There are tons of cool places and ways to pose for pictures and interact with the troll. The most popular way to pose for a picture is to stand on the troll's hand and stick your hand up his nose. However, a reliable source has informed us that in order to be a true Seattleite you must stand on the troll's hand and insert your *head* into the troll's nose!

Some interesting facts about the troll: The troll has never lost a staring contest. The car he is crushing is a real VW

Beetle. The Beetle originally contained a time capsule of Elvis memorabilia.

Paying a visit to the troll can be tons of fun, but be warned that he doesn't really move, so a brief trip will be sufficient. Have no fear, because Fremont is a fun and quirky neighborhood (they have a TROLL!) where there is always something to do!

Downtown Seattle

Olympic Sculpture Park (see "Museums" below)
Location: 2901 Western Ave., Seattle, WA 98121

There are a few notable Seattle pieces that are worth seeing. Most recently Seattle opened the Olympic Sculpture Park. The park is open and free to the public from sunrise to sunset. The park is nine acres and is situated along the waterfront, a beautiful backdrop for sculptures that may call this park their permanent or temporary home. The park boasts eighteen sculptures for public display. A definite Seattle must-see!

Seattle Art Museum (see "Museums" below)
Location: 1300 First Ave., Seattle, WA 98101

No visit to Seattle is complete without seeing Seattle's *Hammering Man* outside the Seattle Art Museum. *Hammering Man*'s arm "hammers" silently and smoothly four times per minute from 7:00 a.m. to 10:00 p.m. every day. It runs on a 3-hp electric motor set on an automatic timer. *Hammering Man* rests his arm each evening and every year on Labor Day.

ART WALKS

In addition to visual art, there are other ways to get your fill of art in Seattle. The biggest Seattle art walk is the first Thursday of every month. The walk resides in Pioneer Square, and more information can be found at: www.firstthursdayseattle.com. The walk gives up-and-coming artists an opportunity to showcase their work to a broad audience. The venues to showcase work can range from a tent propped up in Occidental Park to galleries and artist studios. Take advantage of the map to ensure you don't miss any hidden talent on your tour.

If you missed the first Thursday walk, have no fear, for there is another art walk in Capitol Hill on the second Thursday of every month. Blitz is an arts-oriented open house event that is open from 5:00 p.m. to 8:00 p.m. on the second Thursday of every month. Anywhere between forty and fifty venues will showcase the eclectic arts of Capitol Hill. The types of art range between musical performances, book readings, DJ performances, tastings, and food and beverage specials. To find out more, go to: www.blitzcapitolhill.com.

MUSEUMS

SEATTLE ART MUSEUM
1300 First Ave., Seattle, WA 98101
(206) 654-3100
MON–TUES: Closed
WED: 10:00 a.m.–5:00 p.m.
THURS–FRI: 10:00 a.m.–9:00 p.m.

SAT–SUN: 10:00 a.m.–5:00 p.m.
www.seattleartmuseum.org

Seattle has several popular museums. At the top of this list is the Seattle Art Museum, or the SAM. Located in the heart of downtown Seattle, just north of Pioneer Square and blessed with a beautiful view of Elliott Bay, the SAM is easily recognizable because, well, you just can't miss it. Located on the corner of First Avenue and University Street, it couldn't be more obvious that it is what it is; on the top floor of the five-story building are the words *Seattle Art Museum* engraved into the building itself. The words face University Street and are hard to miss.

Additionally, the museum draws attention to itself because of the *Hammering Man*, a forty-eight-foot-tall steel sculpture of a man hammering. The piece weighs twenty-six thousand pounds and is quite the sight. When the *Hammering Man*, which features a motorized arm, was being erected in 1991, it fell and was damaged and was not successfully installed until 1992 because it had to undergo repairs. The *Hammering Man* is symbolic of Seattle, not only because of its physical presence, but because of what it stands for. The artist, Jonathan Borofsky, says this about his masterpiece and what his vision of it was for Seattle:

> *I want this work to communicate to all the people of Seattle—not just the artists, but families, young and old. I would hope that children who see the* Hammering Man *at work would connect their delight with the potential mysteries that a museum could offer them in their future.*
> *At its heart, society reveres the worker. The* Hammering Man *is the worker in all of us.*

Once inside, prepare to be amazed. There is plenty of natural lighting, which lends itself well to the various exhibits and pieces that are on display. The SAM is known for its diverse collections, especially the Asian, African, Northwest Coast Native American, and modern/contemporary art collections. Additionally, the special exhibitions are great and usually last three to six months.

OLYMPIC SCULPTURE PARK

2901 Western Ave., Seattle, WA 98121
(206) 654-3100
OPEN DAILY: Sunrise–Sunset
www.seattleartmuseum.org/visit/osp

As if the SAM's art pieces and special exhibits weren't enough, the SAM opened a sculpture park in 2007, called the Olympic Sculpture Park. It lies about a mile north of the SAM and sits alongside the Myrtle Edwards Path, which runs along the eastern side of Elliott Bay. There are regularly joggers, runners, walkers, and rollerbladers on the trail, particularly on gorgeous sunny days (not so common here!). The park has eighteen pieces of art; everything there can be seen in under an hour. My favorite sculpture there is comprised of four letters, all randomly placed, and each one barely recognizable: E, O, L, and V. While this might seem obvious, it took me about three visits to the park to look at it and understand that it read LOVE. I appreciate the piece because I feel the artist makes his case perfectly. Yes, love is hard to find and not always recognizable and doesn't always look the way we think it will.

Museum of Glass

1801 Dock St., Tacoma, WA 98402
(866) 468-7386
SUMMER HOURS:
MON–SAT: 10:00 a.m.–5:00 p.m.
SUN: 12:00 p.m.–5:00 p.m.
www.museumofglass.org

Seattle's neighbor to the south, Tacoma, boasts one of the most stunning glass museums in the country: the Museum of Glass, known as the MOG. The MOG's collections are limited to contemporary and Pacific Northwest glass art, and the museum is a hit for visitors as well as locals in the Puget Sound area, partially due to the fact that the well-known glass artist Dale Chihuly's hometown is Tacoma and he has a wide range of both local and international fans and collectors. The Venetian Wall, Crystal Towers, and Seaform Pavilion are all Chihuly masterpieces and big draws to the museum itself.

The MOG, which is comprised of both indoor and outdoor exhibits, is a popular place to visit if you wish to see glassblowing demonstrations. A personal glassblowing friend of mine, James Anderegg, has given demonstrations there and has also studied at Chihuly's own Pilchuck Glass School, an international glass center for glass art education, near Stanwood, Washington. I recently sat down with James in order to get a bit of an insider scoop on the glassblowing scene in and around Seattle; see the "Feature Interview with Local Artist" section of this chapter for details.

LOCAL ARTS CULTURE

In the fall of 2010, the SAM featured an exhibit titled "Kurt," in reference to the late lead singer of the popular nineties Seattle-based grunge band Nirvana. The exhibit was primarily comprised of pieces of work that were inspired by him and documented the impact of his art, his music, and his life. The exhibit was one of the most well-received and well-attended exhibits in SAM's history because of the fact that Cobain has contributed so greatly to the Seattle arts/music scene and culture, and the reverberations of his life live on in so much of the city and its surrounding areas. It is not uncommon to see local churches and other outreach groups market themselves with the popular "Come As You Are" slogan, in reference to Nirvana's hit song of the same name. The song's name captures Seattle's open arms when it comes to drawing in artists of all mediums and kinds; the city (where Cobain lived and ultimately took his own life) will always have an edgy and artsy undertone because of the historical influence of artists, such as Cobain, Jimi Hendrix, Francis Farmer, Dave Matthews, and Eddie Vedder. The culture, style, music scene, and show venues, as well as the unique vibe and art of the various neighborhoods all reveal a uniqueness of their own.

While each neighborhood in Seattle has a different culture as far as the arts scene goes, Capitol Hill is by far the best known when it comes to local music, film, and dance. The area houses many independent theaters, and consequently the majority of Seattle International Film Festival (SIFF) films are viewed there. Overall, Seattle in general and Capitol Hill in particular foster a culture of openness and self-expression.

Kurt Cobain, oil on canvas by "One of Us
Who Doesn't Get Out Often"

Seattle's culture of self-expression is fueled by the various
events and groups that are dedicated to art, in all its forms and
for all tastes and personalities. If you are interested in the writ-
ten or spoken word, there are weekly opportunities to participate in the Seattle Poetry Slam, or yearly in the Seattle Poetry
Festival. Additionally, the ever-popular Elliott Bay bookstore

in Pioneer Square regularly hosts readings and book signings by authors from around the world.

For those who like comedy, Jet City Improv is a must-see venue for a good laugh and is a great experience for up-and-coming comedians. If you are into music, Benaroya Hall, home of the Seattle Symphony, is not to be missed, as musicians and artists of all musical genres perform there weekly. The annual three-day Bumbershoot festival, known for a great lineup of musicians as well as visual art, takes place every Labor Day weekend at the Seattle Center; the festival is well known for featuring primarily indie artists such as Edward Sharpe and the Magnetic Zeroes, Band of Horses, and local Seattle favorite Modest Mouse.

In addition to hosting festivals such as Bumbershoot, the Seattle Center (home of the Space Needle) hosts various events, from concerts to car/boat shows to film festivals to galleries to heritage festivals and arts and crafts shows. A personal favorite of ours is called Urban Craft Uprising, which is Seattle's biggest independent craft show and showcases artists from near and far. Items featured are creative, unique, and handmade and impossible to find elsewhere—this craft show in particular is one of the most inspiring events we've been to...we always walk away with new craft ideas running through our heads, in addition to our purchases, of course!

Seattle, despite having a very defined art scene in terms of events and galleries, also has a thriving scene when it comes to up-and-coming independent artists. The majority of Seattle's coffeehouses showcase local arts in some shape or form, whether by hosting performances by musicians, book readings by authors, or featuring local art. Local Color, an independent coffee shop located in the heart of Pike Place Market, features the work of local artists and rotates an eclectic mix of art on a monthly basis; there you will see paintings, pottery, sculpture, and drawings, in addition to having the opportunity to hear local jazz bands play during certain nights of the week.

While getting around Seattle, you may notice that there are many murals painted; chances are you are looking at the work of local artist Ryan Henry Ward, who signs his work as simply "henry." His artwork can be seen all over the city and is hard to miss. The brightly colored murals often feature quirky characters and are of a whimsical nature. He was recently recognized as one of Seattle's most prominent artists and lives in the Ballard neighborhood of Seattle.

FEATURE INTERVIEW WITH LOCAL ARTIST

James Anderegg was born in 1981 and raised in a suburb east of Seattle, Washington. He is a naturally gifted artist, having started sketching at a young age. In 2002, James was introduced to glassblowing by an acquaintance. He quickly grew interested in the freedom of expression that glass allows and began to hone his skills. In 2007, James attended Pilchuck Glass School for the first time as a way to develop his talent and become exposed to other artists and techniques. James draws inspiration from many things, including nature and random shapes found in everyday life; his desire for creativity and education pushes his art in new directions every day.

Q: How did you get into glassblowing?
A: Glassblowing found me. One of my roommates was a glass-
blower. I started assisting him while he worked. Eventually I
started working for myself to develop my own line of art.

Q: From where do you draw inspiration?
A: I get a lot of my inspiration from street art and tribal or
African sculpture. For the most part, I'll just be sitting there
and something comes to mind. I'll draw it out and then try to
blow it out in glass form.

Resolve

Q: Is there an artist you can relate to?
A: Ethan Stern. We approach glass in a very similar way. I can relate to the way he carves glass.

Q: Who is your favorite artist?
A: Davide Salvadore. I like his form, color use, and playful approach to making glass. He is constantly pushing the boundaries of sculptural form.

Q: What is your favorite piece and why? Do you have any themes you work with regularly?
A: My favorite series from my own line is the Expecting series. I have the opportunity to execute a variety of techniques. With this series, I sit down, put on music, and I just put the piece to the wheel and carve whatever comes to mind. It's never planned. In a sense, it's the truest form of expressing my mind.

Q: How do you intend for your work to be interpreted?
A: I don't make work with forced intentions. I make art to be beautiful and allow viewers to make their own interpretations. For example, in the Expecting series, my vision of it is to express a pregnant woman and all that she has to expect in life. But the viewer of the work may see something completely different, and I welcome that.

Q: How has your work developed throughout the years, and to what or whom do you credit the changes?
A: I have gone from simple forms to more extravagant asymmetrical sculptures. Originally, the color and patterning was applied to the glass hot. Now, once the piece is blown and cooled down, I take the piece to my engraving lathe and carve

the designs and patterns I desire. The biggest help in my development was Greg Dietrich, who taught me cameo engraving, which is the basis for all that I do today. Brian Rubino taught me all I know about proper glassworking techniques.

Q: Can you tell us a little about your experiences at Pilchuck?

A: Pilchuck is a glass school that was founded in 1971. During the summer, it offers two- to three-week courses taught by world-renowned artists and instructors. Since 2007, I have attended every year as a student or teaching assistant. Being in that environment allows me to see people approach glass in so many different ways that I always leave with new ideas on how to move forward with my own work. It's pretty inspiring to have so many creative minds in one place.

Q: What are your favorite glass studios, galleries, etc., in the Seattle area?

A: The galleries that display work I enjoy the most are Traver, Foster White, and Vetri. They display contemporary glass art.

Q: How would you describe the local glassblowing culture?

A: Thriving. There are almost more glassblowers in Seattle than anywhere else in the world. It's a great place to learn about glass and develop your own work.

Q: How do you market yourself, and where can we find your pieces/work in Seattle?

A: Two years ago, I pulled all my work off the market. I have spent that time developing new ideas in glass. I am now at the point where I am ready to show my work.

Q: Where do you want to go with this?
A: I just want to make art. I enjoy blowing glass, and I want to do whatever I can to blow more glass.

From James Anderegg's "Expecting" Series

THEATER

A Very Famous Theatre Company that You Have Most
Definitely Heard Of
Proudly Presents

A Sampling of Seattle Theater

Cast
(in order of appearance)

Tanvi Bhadbhade *(as herself)*
Katy Ardans *(as herself)*
Krsevan Penzar *(as himself)*

Settings

The Paramount Theatre
The Fifth Avenue Theatre
Seattle Musical Theatre
The ACT Theatre

The Paramount Theatre

One of Seattle's oldest theaters, the Paramount has had an interesting albeit checkered life. Like many of the theaters, or "movie palaces" as they were then called, built in the 1920s, the architecture itself is of a fairly dramatic nature. One can imagine Adolf Zukor, movie magnate and then president of Paramount Pictures who led the construction of the theater, instructing the architects, "Boys we don't want any guessing games here. We want the audience to be mesmerized by the surroundings. They should expect nothing but the dramatic once they enter these premises. They step in and ZING-BOOM! They are greeted by beaded chandeliers."

"Beaded chandeliers?" asks the startled architect (one Mr. Rapp), looking slightly worried, once he has descended back to earth from his high jump. "Hmm, beaded chandeliers you say. All right, we will give you beaded chandeliers. But I wish you would stop with those zing-booms! It just wrecks my nerves! Makes me jumpy."

"And lacy iron work, whatever that is. ZING-BANG! Right in front," says Mr. Zukor.

"Ah! I see, I see," says the now slightly more worried looking architect, and gets back to work muttering about zing-bangs being just as bad. Or at least that's how I imagine it would have happened.

In any case, the brothers Rapp delivered, and on March 1, 1928, "The Seattle" greeted its patrons in lavish style. Its interiors were decorated in the French Renaissance style complete with beaded chandeliers, lacy ironwork, gold-leaf-encrusted wall medallions, and hand-loomed French carpeting—and it seated almost four thousand! The main forms of entertainment were vaudeville shows and silent films and not very much later, the "talkies."

In March 1930, the theater changed its name to the Seattle Paramount Theatre. Times were hard because of the Depression, and the theater had to close down in June 1931. However, it reopened in October 1932.

The Paramount had a number of different owners after that. First the Fox Evergreen Corporation tried to turn it into a movie theater (vaudeville shows weren't that popular anymore), even going to the extent of removing 1,600 seats to show Cinerama films, but it wasn't very successful. The theater's popularity declined, and it had to close down again in the 1960s. Some burglars considered this as a personal invitation and paid the theater a visit, leaving it nine paintings (and their gilded frames) short.

Then the Clise Corporation acquired it, renamed it "Paramount Northwest," and decided it had perfect acoustics for rock and jazz concerts. The rock bands and the audience loved the theater, but apparently not its carpets, draperies, and furniture. They jumped on, over, and about these and created quite a mess. Can't say I blame the musicians; it's sort of difficult to rouse your crowd with an anthem while at the same time advocating furniture and carpet maintenance. The brothers Rapp & Rapp clearly did not have a rock concert audience in mind when they designed the theater interiors.

So things continued until in 1981 the Volotin Investment Company bought the Paramount for $1.4 million and tried to spruce it up a bit. The work done on it, though helpful, wasn't adequate, and the theater was in debt again very soon.

Then in 1993 Microsoft vice president Ida Cole bought the Paramount and with the help of some other investors began the work to restore it to its former glory. The newly renovated Paramount Theatre opened its doors on March 16, 1995.

In December 2002, Ida Cole transferred the ownership of the theater to the Seattle Theatre Group, a nonprofit organization, which is its current owner. Today it hosts everything from rock concerts to Broadway shows. So Ninth and Pine would be the way to go, the next time you feel like a Broadway show!

The Fifth Avenue Theatre

The Fifth Avenue Theatre (the Fifth to friends) is located, as the bright ones among you would have cleverly guessed, on Fifth Avenue (1308 Fifth Avenue, to be precise) between University Street and Union Street. In the same peer group as the Paramount Theatre (it opened in 1926), it possesses equally ornate interiors, although in its case the architect decided to give European architecture a miss and go the Oriental route. Interior designer Gustav F. Liljestrom and architect Robert C. Reamer tried to model the interiors of the theater after not one but three of China's architectural wonders: the Forbidden City, the Temple of Heavenly Peace, and the Summer Palace.

One of the things that attracts your attention at once as you enter the theater is the central dome, which has a coiled dragon with a chandelier ("The Pearl of Perfection") suspended from its teeth. For those who have a tendency to get lost, this is an excellent point to keep in mind. Look for the coiled dragon, and if you don't see it, you are in the wrong building. If you are feeling extra cautious, count the toes of the dragon. There should be five (apparently corresponding to five evil spirits that must be vanquished). If there aren't five, then either you are a victim of an elaborate conspiracy designed to fool you into going into a faux–Fifth Avenue theater, or you need to get a pair of glasses.

Other interesting artifacts include a pair of guardian lions modeled after the lions (not real) that stand guard in front of China's imperial palaces. Some sources call them "Foo Dogs," but apparently that is an incorrect term.

Like the Paramount, the Fifth Avenue Theatre served as a venue for vaudeville to begin with and then was turned into a movie palace. It too faced financial difficulties and had to close down in 1978 and narrowly escaped being converted into a Chinese restaurant. However, it was saved due to the efforts of forty-three business leaders who underwrote a $2.6 million loan to save the theater.

Today the Fifth is one of Seattle's most established theaters. It also has a resident theater company called the Fifth Avenue Musical Theatre Company, which was established in 1989 to produce musicals locally so the theater did not have to rely on just the touring Broadway shows. The theater's annual season includes locally produced revivals of classics and touring musicals as well as premieres of shows bound for Broadway.

Another fun fact about the Fifth is that it is considered to be a testing ground for shows before they make their big debut on Broadway. A sort of public beta theater, you could say. This is the reason Seattle audiences were able to catch the musicals *Jekyll & Hyde* and *Hairspray* before they went on to become big hits on Broadway. So the next time you are in the mood for beta testing some Broadway shows, head straight to the Fifth!

Seattle Musical Theatre
Seattle Musical Theatre began as the Civic Light Opera Association, which was formed by a group of opera enthusiasts

in 1978. By 1980 they had moved on from offering operettas and had begun to perform musical theater (which, all things considered, is generally a bit easier to get American crowds interested in). In 2006 they changed their name to Seattle Musical Theatre, and they can currently be found at Magnuson Park Theatre in Northeast Seattle, where they stage all of their productions.

Magnuson Park Theatre is nothing to write home about, but its simplicity allows for a more immersive experience. I'm the type to get distracted by shiny objects, so when a theater is chairs, walls, and a colorful stage and engaging cast, the stage and the cast get my full attention. What's fun is they use the relatively small space to their advantage, working beyond the boundary of the stage when the script allows for it, and filling the room with music from the cast's accompanying live band.

Another thing that SMT does right is their selection of musicals. They are currently performing *The Pajama Game, Hairspray, A Chorus Line,* and *I Love You, You're Perfect, Now Change.* In previous seasons I've seen their productions of *Camelot, The Drowsy Chaperone, Chicago, Company,* and oodles more. In short: their repertoire is across the board, and they even go so far as to stage rarely seen shows such as *110 in the Shade,* the musical version of the film *The Rainmaker.*

Now, musicals aren't for everybody. If you hate fun, you won't like the productions SMT puts on. If you don't like people singing their feelings, you *really* won't like the productions SMT puts on. But if you know you're a fan of musicals, or if you're unsure and want to be convinced, I recommend checking them out. Their Web site has information on their shows and the theater itself, and they're always looking for new talent to bring to the stage.

The ACT Theatre

"DO you believe in me or not!?" bellows the deep and anguished voice of the ghost perusing old Scrooge in front of me. His face is pale, as white as his clothes. Bandages are wrapped around his head. His wild hair sticks out in all directions, like a phantasmal Beethoven. He is bound by chains that stretch from his wrists and ankles to a stage door, and some unknown green smoking hell below. He is wrapped in more chains still, hung with padlocks and coin purses, keys, deeds, coffers, and writs.

Scrooge stammers, "I...I...I believe, Jacob, I believe! S...S...Speak comfort to me!" And betwixt his stammering, globs of spit fly from his mouth. Now Marley is standing a foot from my feet; he points across the round stage to Ebenezer, rattling his chains. As I hear them rattle, not two feet from me, I know them to be made from plastic, and not the rusted iron my mind had imagined.

"You will be visited by three spirits!" the eerie, breath-filled voice warns the shaken Scrooge. Ebenezer screws up his face and looks around the circle theater, facing all sides of the audience. By this, we are to know that visitations from three spirits should hardly be called "comfort." There is an expected chuckle from the onlookers, friends and folks who are entertained by our disdainful protagonist's discomfort.

Some in the crowd know the story well, and their laughter is associated with the guaranteed transformation that our protagonist will undergo. Some are participating in this story of ghosts, generosity, and redemption for the first time.

"EXPECT THE FIRST AT THE STROKE OF ONE!" Jacob Marley calls in his final haunting words, as the trapdoor elevator beneath him draws him into a backstage underworld. A smoke machine from below hurls smoke from his trapdoor and into the round theater. The two brothers sitting in the front row across the stage from me, nine and six years old, look relieved that the imposing ghost has made his exit.

This rendition of Dickens's brilliant *A Christmas Carol* has been a Seattle tradition in my family for over a decade. Its telling, in the round ACT Theatre on Seventh Avenue and Union Street in Seattle, is a staple of our holidays. It runs from Thanksgiving to Christmas Eve each year, and it is highly recommended.

MUSIC

So, as you might have heard, we don't get out much. But how can we ignore one of the most exciting music scenes in the country? Resistance is futile, and heck—sometimes we have to get ourselves out of the office, off the couch, or away from our phone and computer screens to feel the thumping vibrations of some live music. Man and woman cannot live on iPods alone.

For much of its existence, Seattle has been an overlooked corner of the country. And yet, somehow, that's incubated a surprisingly strong and diverse music culture in the overcast Puget Sound. From Gypsy Rose Lee and Bing Crosby to Ray Charles and Quincy Jones, from the Wailers and the Sonics to Jimi Hendrix and Heart, from Robert Cray and the Ventures to Sir Mix-a-Lot and Queensrÿche, from Soundgarden and Nirvana to Modest Mouse and Death Cab for Cutie—Seattle and the Pacific Northwest have never been a place to stay at home just because it's raining outside.

Once you finally drag yourself out into the gray drizzle, you'll probably realize that there is far more music to experience in Seattle than one day, or even a long weekend, will allow. One discovery will inevitably lead to another band, venue, or event—in a place perhaps two or three degrees removed from anything featured in this guide. And that, essentially, is part of the Emerald City's charm: music really *is* nearly everywhere.

Some reminders of the past are in plain sight (the **statue of Hendrix** on Broadway in Capitol Hill), while others are a mecca to die-hard fans (**Jimi's grave** in Renton). Fans of the still influential *and* oft-reviled grunge era (http://en.wikipedia.org/wiki/Grunge) continue to drive down Lake Washington Boulevard for a glimpse of **Kurt and Courtney's house**—or swing through the Pioneer Square area to visit the spots and blocks where the "Seattle scene" of the late eighties and early nineties bloomed.

One (rich) fan—Paul Allen—turned his dream of a museum honoring Jimi Hendrix into the broader **Experience Music Project**, a massive, Frank Gehry–designed sculpture of a building full of rock music exhibitions and memorabilia with a focus on said guitar slinger, along with the many other artists of the Pacific Northwest. An exhibit chronicling the full career of Nirvana has been a recent success. And if a full tour of Seattle appeals to you, consider purchasing a discounted "CityPass" that will get you into **EMP**, plus many other attractions: http://www.empmuseum.org/visit/index.asp?categoryID=160.

SHOPPING FOR MUSIC

One could also while away an entire day browsing around Seattle's many record stores. For all of the modern advances in digital music, Seattle still boasts a variety of homegrown shops for you to get your hands on the latest local and national product. **Easy Street Records** and **Sonic Boom** have branched out across the city and get the word out about new music with frequent in-store appearances by local and touring artists (you might also notice a few local artists working behind the counter). And smaller shops such as **Singles Going Steady** in Belltown, **Jive Time** in Fremont, and **Wall of**

Sound in Capitol Hill specialize in vinyl treasures and hard-to-find releases typically deserving of their own large window displays. And don't forget to ask the helpful clerks about local record labels to get yourself a listen to some music you might be interested in seeing out and about town. There's **Sub Pop,** of course. The label that introduced grunge to the world and "put Seattle on the map" is still cranking out quality acts after a new-century shift to the more indie side of the music palate, or even hip-hop for that matter, while their new-ish imprint, **Hardly Art,** brings hardly typical, arty-underground bands to your attention. Another heavy-hitter in the indie genre would be **Barsuk Records,** discoverers of Death Cab for Cutie. New labels like **Mt. Fuji** can point you to the new scene happening in the smaller clubs around town, while others like **Suicide Squeeze** and **Tooth & Nail** keep the long-running punk scene fresh. Jazz and the avant-garde are also maintaining a strong pulse in today's Seattle via established outlets such as **Origin Records**—and young labels such as **Tables & Chairs,** and the vibrant scene that sprouted them—which was featured in the *New York Times* in 2010: http://www.nytimes.com/2010/08/29/arts/music/29seattle.html.

Or maybe you're interested in making your own noise. With every other person you bump into on the street in Seattle being a musician, someone's got to be furnishing them with instruments, right? Besides the usual national chains, if you look closely you'll notice some great specialists right under your nose. For vintage equipment enthusiasts, there's the **Trading Musician** in Ravenna and **Emerald City Guitars** in Pioneer Square. For rockers with cash to burn, go see **Randy Parsons** in South Lake Union—he might be able to squeeze you in for a handcrafted guitar as soon as he's done with the ones Jimmy

Page and Jack White are waiting for. If it's volume you need, **Ben Verellen** has been providing the loudest metal bands on the West Coast with gorgeous, wood-paneled amplifiers from his small shop in Fremont. Conversely, if acoustic sounds rule your world, turn to Fremont's longtime **Dusty Strings** emporium. And no matter your interests and/or obsessions, remember: talk to the folks behind the counter. You may find yourself flooded with not only highly valuable shopping tips but also a laundry list of bands to check out and spots to hit—to hear and see all that gear in glorious action.

VENUES AND FESTS

After all, it's all about live music in a town like Seattle. No matter what your preferences—rock, pop, punk, jazz, avant-garde, hip-hop, electronic, DJs, dance parties, and everything in between—there's something for you in just about every neighborhood.

For national touring acts, a variety of larger venues cater to the big crowds. The **WaMu Theater** by the stadium in SoDo, the **Key Arena** in lower Queen Anne, and **Tacoma Dome** down south provide the larger-scale environment and nearby convenience to catch big acts as they pass through the Northwest.

Mid-sized venues such as the **Paramount Theatre**, the **Moore Theatre**, the **Showbox** (at the Market or in SoDo), or **Neumos** in Capitol Hill provide a more intimate experience for seeing your favorite touring acts up close. And similarly sized outdoor destinations such as **Concerts at Marymoor**

(Park) or Chateau Ste. Michelle provide sublime summer nights under our cloudy stars.

But the finest fun and adventure can be found by hitting the smaller local clubs or bars, where the divide between musician and audience melts away. The **Crocodile** in Belltown remains one of the premiere small-to-mid-sized clubs where you can catch local and touring indie up-and-comers. Other good bets for that indie music the kids go for include the **Sunset** on Ballard Avenue and the **High Dive** in Fremont. If you're into something louder and harsher—or maybe smellier—you can find some rock, metal, and punk at the classic dive the **Comet** in Capitol Hill, or the **Funhouse** under the monorail next to Seattle Center. For more of a funky vibe, try **Nectar** or the **White Rabbit** in Fremont, along with Wallingford's **Seamonster Lounge**. For some twang, there's always the famous **Tractor Tavern** or **Conor Byrne** in Ballard for a night of Americana, singer-songwriters, and the like—or Greenlake's **Little Red Hen** for a night of lively country tunes. And on the jazzy side, national acts are the norm at Belltown's **Jazz Alley**.

For local acts, turn to the nearby **Tula's**, the **New Orleans Creole Restaurant** in Pioneer Square, or **Egan's Jam House** in Ballard. Or, if sittin' down is out of the question and house-shakin' party DJs are your thing, keep an eye on nightclubs such as **Trinity** or the **Last Supper Club** in Pioneer Square—and the highly trafficked and diverse **NWTekno.org** community hub. Lastly, the **Triple Door** offers up nearly everything but punk rock at its gorgeous-looking and gorgeous-sounding restored vaudeville-era downtown theater, located just across the street from **Benaroya Hall** (the home of the Seattle Symphony). And if you're feeling even more adventurous and stealthy, keep your ears open for underground rock 'n' beyond shows at the

Josephine, Healthy Times Fun Club, Black Lodge—or none of these, for that matter, as these "venues" come and go as rents go up or tenants move on. For the latest news and links from this ever-shifting world of spaces and houses, visit **SeattleDIY.com**. (Disclaimer: sites disappear as well, and that's where Google comes in!) And for a good overview of the numerous aboveground venues in town, check out local movers 'n' shakers **KEXP** radio, and their lengthy club guide: http://kexp.org/events/clublist.asp.

And for those of us who *really* don't get out much, there are festivals. Take care of a year's worth of shows in one shot! Over the course of a day or a long weekend, Seattle provides many great opportunities to catch a ton of music and performance in a festival atmosphere. With a clear understanding of the winter weather patterns in the Northwest, most promoters schedule their festivals during the warmer and clearer summer months. A newcomer (in the past ten years) that has become an instant favorite is the **Sasquatch Festival**, held at the picturesque Columbia River Gorge in central Washington (George, to be exact). Geared toward the indie music scene, Sasquatch does a great job of balancing national headliners with many local acts. The I-90 exodus from Seattle begins on Friday night as festivalgoers vie for the best local accommodations or to stake out a camping spot for the weekend. Moreover, the once-nascent **Capitol Hill Block Party** is also firmly on the radar, offering a raucous mix of local, regional, and national acts with a focus on lively, hipster-friendly rock/punk/pop, hip-hop, dance/DJ acts spread out over a full weekend every July.

Another recently founded and rapidly growing event that's centered in Capitol Hill is the **Decibel Fest**, a carefully curated happening featuring electronic and DJ music spanning a wide spectrum of style and scene. Acts arrive from all over the world, and, increasingly, so do fans. Also impressive in its genre-spanning breadth is the veteran **Earshot Jazz Festival**, held over a three-week period every fall in venues both big and tiny. If you're staying in town for the Memorial Day weekend, **Northwest Folklife** is a long-running (and donation-based!) alternative (for more information on this festival, see the "Only in Seattle" chapter). For forty years, the Folklife Festival has taken over Seattle Center underneath the Space Needle to celebrate folk, ethnic, international, and traditional arts with a crunchy heap of music—from bands to buskers to drum circles to dancing—to keep you entertained. Lastly, the granddaddy of all Seattle festivals—**Bumbershoot**—caps off the summer on Labor Day weekend. A wee bit older than Folklife and many times the size, Bumbershoot attracts over one hundred thousand people to catch hundreds of performances over the weekend in dozens of Seattle Center venues, indoor and out. Artists have ranged from huge draws like Bob Dylan and Eminem to local acts like the Decemberists and Modest Mouse playing before their earliest festival audiences. If there's one weekend to get your music fix in Seattle, Bumbershoot is probably it—no matter what your taste. But if ukuleles, bagpipes, or noise is your *only* thing, so to speak, there's a fest out there for you. Seattle hosts a tremendous number of smaller and/or niche-oriented showcases as well.

MUSIC NEWS AND EVENTS

Which leads us to Seattle's best event calendars, listings, and the like. For general purposes, our two free alternative-weeklies tower over all other sources and are available at countless street corners, coffee shops, and bars. *The Stranger* (http://www.thestranger.com/seattle/Music) and *Seattle Weekly* (http://www.seattleweekly.com/music) are comprehensive in scope, especially when viewed online, and their respective music blogs serve as essential companion sites: late-breaking show announcements, ticket on-sales, and nightly show recommendations are commonplace. Be sure to bookmark *The Stranger*'s LINE OUT (http://lineout.thestranger.com/blogs/lineout) and the *Seattle Weekly*'s REVERB (http://blogs.seattleweekly.com/reverb), especially if you're prone to making last-minute plans. Also free, and widely available, is the *City Arts* glossy—featuring timely arts/music articles and event details (http://www.cityartsonline.com). Keep an eye out for smaller, and typically genre-focused, complimentary publications as well—such as *Earshot Jazz* (http://earshot.org) and *All About Jazz*–Seattle (http://www.allaboutjazz.com/seattle/index.html). Lastly, we must not forget about KEXP 90.3 and their truly multifaceted Web site—perhaps the best of any radio station there is (http://www.kexp.org/events).

Speaking of Web sites, if you're worried about getting your fingers inky—this *is* the twenty-first century—Seattle's music blogs continue to grow in number and influence. The sparkly **Three Imaginary Girls** have built up a hub for all things indie pop, while **Seattle Rock Guy** keeps his features dark and heavy. **Sound on the Sound, Seattle Subsonic, SSG Music,** and the *Seattle Times* newspaper's **Matson on Music** are some other popular, well-rounded feeds—and a myriad of others too numerous to mention are out there, including genre-specific ones such as **206up.com, Seattle Jazz Scene,** and the aforementioned **NWTekno.** Check out the many audio, video, and podcast links along with their many connections to other blogs (namely "blogrolls," and note that 206up has posted quite a cool selection of recommendations). Explore away, and you'll be rewarded with up-to-the-minute scoops, especially if you branch out and like/follow the Facebook pages and Twitter accounts run by most of these bloggers. And again—don't sleep on **KEXP** (http://blog.kexp.org/blog).

Seattle is also lucky to have local radio that keeps homegrown music in focus. Former UW college radio station KCMU was picked up and provided additional funding by Paul Allen's EMP, becoming **KEXP** 90.3 FM. They air many themed shows covering all major genres, along with indispensable local programming like *Audioasis* on Saturday nights, which showcases live events often broadcast directly from Seattle's venues. **KBCS** 91.3 also features genre-specific and local-music-driven shows. Moreover, **KNDD** has been promoting local bands since the grunge boom, while **KISW**'s show *Loud and Local* can hip you to some of the heavier acts around town. And longstanding NPR station **KPLU** covers all things jazz and blues—while **C89.5** kicks out nonstop dance/DJ music, and, like all of the above, sponsors lots of local events.

In sum, the music's out there. In abundance. And, like stations on the dial, it's not hard to find: all you have to do is think of your favorite style of music, and there's a venue or event out there for you. Visit the sites mentioned here, browse the tons of Seattle music event listings on Facebook, search Twitter for "Seattle" + "music," and network with friends—but you could certainly disregard all of this, pick a neighborhood, poke around, and stumble upon some fun tunes nearby. After all, this is legendary Seattle, "City of Music." (If you do only one thing, peruse this: http://seattlecityofmusic.com.)

PROFESSIONAL SPORTS

THE OLD BALL GAME: SEATTLE MARINERS

There is nothing better to do on a glorious Seattle summer evening than taking in a Seattle Mariners game at Safeco Field, affectionately known as "The Safe" by many Mariners faithful. The sights, sounds, and smells of the ballpark have an uncanny way of bringing one back to fond childhood memories.

Before entering the park you must buy a ticket. If money is no object, we would suggest going with the Diamond Club seats, the first few rows right behind home plate. With the tickets you get a private entrance and all the food and beverages you can ingest—all for the modest price of about $300 per ticket. But you can't go wrong with any seats in the house. The center field bleacher seats are $7 and on sunny summer nights are covered in sun for at least an hour. If you're going to the game to be more social than avid, buy the cheap seats and hang out with your friends on field level in the beer garden. It is packed with people who are more into sipping suds and talking than watching. The best value is the outfield reserve seating. Pick a right field seat as close to the field as possible, and you will feel like part of the game.

Now that your ticket is purchased, you will no doubt need a pre-game plan. Save yourself some hassle and catch the light rail or bus to the game. It drops you off a five-minute walk from the stadium for a fraction of the cost of gas and parking. Before entering the park, take a walk down Occidental Avenue. Here you will find a cornucopia of street vendors and performers. You will smell freshly popped kettle corn and brats on the grill. If you want to eat, you will find the best value near the stadium here. You may also want to pick up some peanuts, licorice, or Cracker Jacks from a vendor, as prices inside are at least triple. With a full stomach, head toward the stadium and cross First Avenue to Pyramid Brewery. Grab a beer at the beer garden and get ready to take in the game.

If you are visiting "The Safe" for the first time, walk south on First until you come to Edgar Martinez Drive. The home plate entrance on the corner is the grandest entrance in the park.

If you're a more serious fan, or coming to the ballpark with the family, skip the beer garden and head in early. Gates open two hours before first pitch, which usually allows time to see some batting practice. Head to the right field bleachers for your best shot at catching a BP home run ball for a souvenir. If you are hungry, you will be surprised at the selection of food. If you have a craving for it, there is a good chance you can find it. Don't forget to save room for the famous garlic fries, a Safeco Field tradition.

SCARVES UP: SEATTLE SOUNDERS

It starts with the march to the match. Seattleites clad in blue and green, scarves draped across their shoulders. Dooom! Dooom! Dooom! Somewhere up front a bass drum keeps the beet of the march. And a chant begins:

"Oh to! Oh to be! Oh to be a Sounder!"

The voices ripple backwards, and then I'm chanting, and you're chanting next to me. Before long the chant gives way to song:

"When it's us versus them, you can always count on me!
When it's us versus them, it's a Sounders unity!"

As we walk through Pioneer Square, more and more trickle in and join our number. We are the Seattle river of green and blue, flowing towards Qwest. As we pass by pubs and bars, patrons raise up half-emptied beer glasses or pitchers. Green Sounders flags hang from the windows. Cheers and hollers come from inside; the pregame MLS coverage flashes on flat screens behind.

We are in the stadium now, and every seat is filled. The fans are on their feet. To my left, at the south end behind the goal, sit the heart of our supporters. They chant and cheer furiously. They wave flags of green and blue and black, shouting, "Scarves up!" and every hand in the stadium grabs the end of a green scarf and raises it heavenward. By this sign our footballers know they're home, and our opponents are warned that this will be a difficult pitch from which to draw a point.

The game is tough; there is a tussle for every ball. Zakuani has got the ball on the left wing; he passes a defender and is running towards two more. He passes ball up and center, Montero has it! A defender plants himself in front of Fredy and takes the ball; the opposing team starts to move into the offensive. But then Brad Evans comes in from outta the sky! His brilliant dribbling skills win us the ball; he passes it quickly and precisely to Lamar Neagle, at the top of the box now, unlikely position. But wait! The defenders are dazed, they look a little lost—there is an opening! He lets it rip and GOOOAA AAALLLLLLLLLLLLLLLLLLLLLLLLL!

The stadium erupts! Hugs and high fives for everybody.

OUTDOORS

Puget Sound is host to a wide variety of outdoor activities, thanks to its geography. From oceans to lakes, beaches to mountains, and planned parks to untouched forests, living in the Northwest can provide a virtually inexhaustible list of things to do outside. A topic on just one activity could easily span one or more books, so in this chapter we'd like to present you with just a few things we like to do in the sometimes sunny, sometimes rainy, always fun area of Seattle.

SKIIING/SNOWBOARDING

Seattle is well known for its rainy and gloomy days, but look at it from the bright side—rain in Seattle usually means snow in the mountains. The Pacific Northwest offers a wide variety of terrain in the Cascade and Olympic Mountains with breathtaking winter scenery and mountaintop views. Relaxed slopes, steep runs, un-groomed glades, and rugged backcountry attract snow sport fans of any level.

According to data from the National Ski Areas Association, Washington State has sixteen ski resorts. Here is a short review of three resorts, each a jewel on its own.

THE SUMMIT AT SNOQUALMIE

1001 State Route 906, Snoqualmie Pass, WA 98068
(425) 434-7669
www.summitatsnoqualmie.com

Located within an easy hour's drive from Seattle, the Summit at Snoqualmie appeals to all of us who worship additional wholesome sleep in the morning. This resort consists of four mountains: Summit Central sports a terrain park and half-pipe; Summit East looks like the place to escape the crowds; Summit West welcomes beginners; and Alpental, the giant among them, is loved for its backcountry.

CRYSTAL MOUNTAIN RESORT

33914 Crystal Mountain Blvd., Crystal Mountain, WA 98022
(360) 663-2265
www.crystalmountainresort.com

Located eighty-two miles southeast of Seattle, serious skiers and boarders enjoy spring and summer skiing into July at Crystal Mountain. Crystal Mountain is Washington's largest ski area, offering everything you can think of: nighttime skiing or snowboarding, downhill slopes, powder runs and tree skiing, a terrain park that includes a half-pipe, and usually great snow conditions topped off with a beautiful view of Mount Rainier.

STEVENS PASS
Summit Stevens Pass, U.S. Hwy. 2, Skykomish, WA 98288
(206) 812-4510
www.stevenspass.com

Stevens Pass, about eighty miles east of Seattle, is split into front and back sides. The resort offers a variety of trails ranging from green to double black, with the majority of these runs beautifully groomed and wide open for long, cruising runs. The back side has many options for adventurous folks who prefer to go off the beaten trail and play around in unattended terrain. Night skiing and Springfest, which takes place during the last weekend of the season, make for lots of great memories.

A piece of advice: Don't borrow a friend's season pass to save on a day ticket. Season passes have pictures of the owner, and the operators carry out random checks. It gets nasty when you get caught. Also, it really isn't classy!

Kill Three Birds with One Stone!

1. Hiking up a secret mountain to be the first one to hit that powder works your legs. Digging yourself out after you've plummeted into fifteen inches of fresh snow is better core work than P90X. Get your muscles warmed up with fifty push-ups before hitting the slopes, **and you are ready for the beach once summer comes!**

2. Granted, skiing and snowboarding are expensive hobbies. Here is some advice for how you can actually **save money:** pay up front for a season pass, find a group of people who are as passionate as you to carpool with, and then hit the mountain every Saturday and Sunday. You will be so tired at night that all you'll want to do is get a good night's sleep. Have you ever added up everything you spend on drinks, movies, and clubs during an entire winter season? It's probably more than the cost of a season pass.

3. Whether you're elegantly curving down the hill, somersaulting, or gliding on your bottom, it is **pure fun!** There is simply no better way to spend your time.

SCUBA DIVING

Sometimes when people talk about SCUBA diving, they talk only about tropical reefs and brightly colored fish that are found far away from the gray skies of Seattle. What some people are surprised to hear, however, is that the Pacific Coast of North America has some of the best diving in the world, and the relatively protected water of Puget Sound is no exception. As soon as you submerge yourself, you are greeted by an environment teeming with life. On every dive you're almost guaranteed to see cod, cabezon, nudibranchs, jellyfish, sea stars, crabs, and plumose anemones. Puget Sound is also home to the giant Pacific octopus, the largest octopus in the world.

The Alki Coves

Located in West Seattle, the coves at Alki Beach are probably the most accessible dive sites in the Seattle area. There are three coves in all, referred to (surprisingly enough) as Alki Cove 1, Alki Cove 2, and Alki Cove 3. There is ample street parking near all the coves and a parking lot at Cove 2, near the water taxi and fish-and-chips restaurant.

The coves provide easy shore access dives, with very little worry about current. Because of this, these coves are a popular location for classes on the weekends. You'll probably see lots of other divers on the shore during the warmer months, but in general everyone is friendly, and it's not crowded once you get underwater anyway. Also, if you're lacking a dive buddy, Cove 2 is a good place to meet up with people.

There is a lot to see at the shallower depths, mainly plumose anemones clinging to the old submerged piers and crabs scurrying around the bottom. At Cove 2 at around thirty-five to forty feet depth, there is a small sunken boat called the *Honey Bear*. I've heard an octopus makes its lair around there, and although I've seen a lot of what looks like the remains of its meals (old shells), I've never managed to see it.

Directions: From I-5, take the West Seattle Bridge to Harbor Avenue SW. Travel north on Harbor Avenue SW. Cove 1 is next to Salty's Restaurant. Cove 2 is just before the fish-and-chips restaurant and water taxi dock. Cove 3 is just past the restaurant and dock.

Alki Pipelines

Just around the corner from the Alki Coves is another dive site named after pipelines that stretch out from the shore at Beach Drive SW. This site is still a fairly easy dive, but it's a bit more exposed than the Alki Coves, so it's usually less populated with beginners due to some minor current and occasionally more choppiness at the surface.

There are two pipelines here: a large diameter pipe that runs out southwest from the shore and a smaller diameter one that runs almost directly west from the shore. Each hosts a variety of life along and around its surface, which makes for leisurely and easily navigated dives. The smaller pipe is exposed during low tide, so it is easy to find.

The larger pipe is buried until farther out but is still easy to find. Just enter the water straight out from the circular platform between the ramp and the last residential building on the beach, and then head almost directly southwest once submerged. You'll know you're on the right track when you see a garden gnome on the bottom. Yes, a garden gnome. He is your guide, telling you to continue to head southwest from him a bit farther. Soon you'll see more plant life, and a bit farther along the large pipe will emerge from the bottom. Again, lots of life to see, and I've heard that another elusive octopus lives around here.

You can swim all the way to the end of the pipe and peer into the shadowy opening. Although I wouldn't recommend it, a buddy of mine and I dared each other to enter the pipe. I scared myself when I finally worked up the courage just to swim partially into it. The light from my large flashlight was just swallowed up by the darkness and I couldn't see anything. I turned around and came out very quickly. My shame didn't last long since my buddy chickened out completely.

Directions: From I-5, take the West Seattle Bridge to Harbor Avenue SW. Follow Harbor Avenue SW around the point. The road name will become Alki Avenue SW. Continue to follow the road heading southwest until you come to a three-way stop at Sixty-third Avenue SW. Make a left onto Sixty-third Avenue SW, heading south. As the road curves left, turn right onto Beach Drive SW. The beach is right there.

Edmonds Underwater Park

Located at a small beach right beside the Kingston–Edmonds Ferry dock at Edmonds, this popular site has it all. On the surface there is a beach, a lookout, changing rooms, restrooms, and an outdoor shower for the divers. Under the surface it's...well, a dive park. Sunken boats, tires, pilings—if it's sinkable, it's probably there, creating man-made reef structures to be home for all sorts of life. The park has mapped routes by fixed guide ropes along the bottom, which is great for navigation and discovering all the cool stuff around here.

Be sure to say in-bounds of the park, especially since there is a passenger ferry right beside you. There is a sign near the ferry to warn you.

There is a parking lot, but the spaces fill up fast on the weekends. Make sure to get there early to get a parking spot. If the lot is full, your other option is to drop your buddy and the gear at the beach and find road parking a few blocks away.

Directions: Take I-5 to Edmonds, and follow the signs to the Kingston Ferry (on Route 104, which eventually becomes Edmonds Way). Stay out of the ferry lanes. Turn left at the intersection for the ferry and an immediate right into Brackett's Landing and parking lot.

The opportunity for diving around Seattle is great, and there are many more sites than the ones I mentioned here. If you are really interested in SCUBA diving in this area, there is a great book that practically every diver I know owns, *Northwest Shore Dives* by Stephen Fischnaller. You can also head to your local dive shops as divers are usually a friendly bunch who like to share information and their experiences. Two shops I can recommend are Underwater Sports and the Lighthouse Diving Center. Underwater Sports has seven locations in Puget Sound, Bellevue, Edmonds, Federal Way, Kirkland, Olympia, Seattle, and Tacoma.

SAILING IN SEATTLE

Seattle has much to offer in terms of water sports. Surrounded by lakes and Puget Sound, access to the water is easy and open to everyone. Sailors of every level have many affordable ways to get out onto the water.

Lake Washington is to the east of downtown. The water is warm enough for swimming in the summer, and Seattle Parks and Recreation offers sailing lessons and boat rentals from the Mount Baker facility in Seward Park. The winds are typically light and pleasant for the casual sailor, and there is a series of races on Tuesday and Wednesday nights from the docks at Leschi.

Lake Union and Portage Bay are part of the waterways that connect Lake Washington to Puget Sound and are right in the heart of the city. Seattle Yacht Club sits in a historic building in the Montlake area and provides sailing lessons in small boats to the public in the summer. On Lake Union, sailors have a great view of downtown and the houseboats that line the lake. The Center for Wooden Boats, located at the south end of the lake, rents larger sailboats, and also offers lessons in the summer.

Farther to the west, under the dramatic Olympic Mountains, is Puget Sound, a saltwater sea that connects to the Strait of Juan de Fuca and the Pacific Ocean approximately sixty miles north of Seattle. Puget Sound is about three miles across, one hundred miles long, and the winds are typically stronger than on the lake. In the winter, the winds come from the south, bringing rain and weather. In the summer, the winds come from the north, usually in the afternoon, bringing sunshine and white clouds. The water is a constant 48 degrees, so sailors need to be prepared for colder winds, even in the summer. Corinthian Yacht Club offers sailing lessons at Shilshole Marina, as does Seattle Sailing Club, which charters small keelboats. There are races on many weekends throughout the year and in the evenings in the summer.

It is hard to travel around the city and not see some bit of water or mountains in Seattle. Sailing is a great way to experience the water and take advantage of the natural beauty that surrounds us.

OUTDOOR RUNNING

Seattle is notorious for its continuous rain and gray skies. Interestingly, this provides the best environment for outdoor running. You never get too hot or too thirsty. In addition, you will find a lot of people running outside, encouraging you. Once you finish your running, you will feel better and that you've accomplished more than just running because you just ran through the rain. Also, running is a great sport because you can do it by yourself or with your friends.

Each year, Seattle hosts numerous running events, including the well-known Seattle Marathon and the Seattle Rock 'n' Roll Marathon. Following is a list of fun and well-organized running events for each month.

Month	Race Name	Distance	Location
January (1/1)	Resolution Run	5K	Magnuson Park, Seattle, WA
February (around 2/14)	Love 'em or Leave 'em Valentine's Day Dash	5K	Green Lake Park, Seattle, WA
March (around 3/20)	Mercer Island Half Marathon	Half Marathon	Mercer Island, WA
April (around 4/9)	Skagit Valley Tulip Run	2mi/5mi	Burlington, WA
May (around 5/1)	Top Pot Doughnuts 5K	5K	Seattle, WA
June (around 6/25)	Seattle Rock 'n' Roll Marathon and 1/2	Half/Full Marathon	Seattle, WA
July (around 7/16)	Chelan Man Half Marathon	10K/Half	Lake Chelan, WA
August (around 8/21)	Lake Union 10K	10K	Lake Union, Seattle, WA
September (around 9/25)	Fremont Oktoberfest Brew Ha Ha 5K	5K	Fremont, Seattle, WA
October (around 10/9)	Portland Marathon	Half/Full Marathon	Portland, OR

Month	Race Name	Distance	Location
November (around 11/27)	Seattle Marathon	Half/Full Marathon	Seattle Center, Seattle, WA
December (around 12/11)	Seattle Jingle Bell Run	5K	Westlake Center, Seattle, WA

You don't have to sign up for running events to enjoy outdoor running. Here is the list of outdoor trails you can try even during your lunchtime, after work, or over the weekend. All of the below trails have views of the beautiful lake or the bay. How amazing it is!

Location	Distance	Difficulty	Comments
Seward Park, Seattle, WA	2.5mi	Easy	Paved loop trail with great lake Washington view.
Alki Beach Park, Seattle, WA	2.5mi	Easy	From Alki point to Duwamish Head on Elliott Bay. Paved trail with Elliott Bay view. You can see beach volleyball players during the summer season.
Green Lake, Seattle, WA	2.7mi	Easy	Paved loop trail with great view over Green Lake.

Location	Distance	Difficulty	Comments
Discovery Park, Seattle, WA	2.8mi	Medium	Unpaved natural loop trail with great view over Elliott Bay.
Lake Union, Seattle, WA	6.2mi	Easy	Paved loop trail with great view over Lake Union and downtown.
East Lake Sammamish, WA	11mi	Easy	From Marymoor Park in Redmond to Gilman Boulevard in Issaquah. Partially paved trail with great view of Lake Sammamish and beautiful luxurious houses.

"But I don't even have a pair of running shoes," you say. Don't worry. You can always buy running shoes online using Amazon.com, Endless.com (free shipping and free return), or Zappos.com (free shipping and free return). Or you can try local running specialty stores in the Green Lake area.

One critical piece of gear that I recommend for outdoor running in Seattle is a running cap. If you have a breathable hooded T-shirt, that will do as well. Even if your day starts with beautiful sunshine, you never know when it will start raining. It is always smart to bring your running cap.

Now, are you ready to run?

SEATTLE BY BIKE

The best way to see Seattle is on a bike. When exploring on foot, the ground you cover is limited, and by car, it's just plain dangerous and expensive. On a bus, you are at risk of getting sick, and on a boat you may get wet.

The cycling community in the Northwest is arguably one of the best in the country. Our moderate climate contributes to the opportunity to ride and compete year round. The best time to compete is in the autumn when the leaves are changing, there is a chill in the air, and mud on the ground. It is cyclocross season!

Driving up to the parking lot you see the yellow tape marking the course, hear cowbells ringing in the distance, and there is the beer garden in the center of it all. It is raining. Of course. It's Seattle.

As I get my bike out of my car and strap on my mountain bike shoes, the chill of the air matches the chill of my nerves. I am ready to get muddy and anticipate my trophy at the end...a nice cold local Northwest microbrew. I line up at the starting line surrounded by familiar faces that are all excited to hear the whistle blow. The whistle blows, and we are off. Suddenly mud is splashing into my eyes, the rain begins to pour, and my legs begin to burn. The race is on, and my nerves finally begin to calm.

It is the sense of community and the rush that makes me love this sport. The Northwest is the ideal place to host this crazy love to bike.

MOTORCYCLE TRACKS

Many people aren't aware of one of Seattle's greatest attractions: motorcycle tracks. Rain or shine, the tracks are open to ride. Before we talk about the tracks themselves, we first need to talk about the things you'll need:

1. Motorcycle
    a. Coolant switch (WaterWetter or water)
    b. Remove all glass (tape up plastic)

2. Gear
   a. Riding boots
   b. Gauntlet gloves
   c. Leather jacket
   d. Leather pants
   e. Chest protector
   f. Helmet
3. Cooler/food/water
4. Camera (to show your friends all your cool pictures)
5. Friends (to help you get your bike there)

Once you have these things, you'll have the essential items needed to ride your motorcycle at the track.

Now that your bike is all ready, you'll need to find a track in the Seattle area to ride. Listed below are a few raceways:

1. Pacific Race Way
   31001 144th Ave. SE, Kent, WA 98042
   (253) 639-5927
   www.pacificraceways.com
2. The Ridge Motorsports Park (Coming in 2012)
   West Eells Hill Rd. NE, Shelton, WA, 98765
   www.ridgemotorsportspark.com
3. Spokane Raceway Park (Spokane, WA)
   North 102 Hayford Rd., Spokane, WA 99224
   (509) 244-3663
   www.spokaneracewaypark.com

Each track has particular track days and times, so you'll want to investigate further for when and where works for you.

The Top Five Must-Have Items to Survive the Outdoors, Seattle-Style

People often view the outdoors and the city as two different worlds, two separate realms on entirely opposite ends of the spectrum. One is marked by untamed wilderness and the forces of nature, the other by human civilization and advanced infrastructure. Fresh air and muddy trails on one side, paved roads and free public Wi-Fi access on the other.

Well, up here in Seattle we don't get that distinction. And the first time you walk into a pack of raccoons spilling the contents of your trash cans all over the driveway, you'll wholeheartedly agree: to step outside of your house in Seattle is to step into the Great Outdoors. This includes (on many, many days of the year) constant rain, wildly fluctuating temperatures, and changing seasons (sorry to all folks from California). So to help you brave the Seattle outdoors in style—whether you're hiking up Mount Rainier or walking to the office from the parking lot—here's a list of "Five Must-Have Items" that will make your life a whole lot easier, and more comfy:

1. **Lightweight outer shell rain jacket (hooded).** A deeply rooted Seattle cliché maintains that only tourists use umbrellas around here, which may or may not be true. But ultimately, a lightweight, rain-repellent outer shell jacket is not only easier to pack and carry along at all times—it will also leave both of your hands free for exciting things like rock climbing or drinking coffee (see 2). This jacket will be your best friend and a constant companion year-round, because it does rain a lot in these parts, although the rain is more of a constant drizzle at most times, not the kind of torrential downpour that would warrant an umbrella. Also note: while black seems to be a very "of the moment" color choice right now, bright colors like yellow, orange, or green will make you more noticeable as a pedestrian, especially on those drizzly days when visibility on the streets is low.

2. **Take-out coffee cup (preferably steaming hot).** Seattle coffee conglomerates are credited for introducing the subtleties of gourmet coffee to a globalized audience. In the process, they have also made the paper take-out coffee cup a ubiquitous sight around the world. In Seattle, these cups perform double duty as mobile hand-warmers and sources of constant comfort on overcast days. When skies are gray and the streets turn into rivers, cradling your hands around a steaming cup of java or tea is the closest thing to the soothing warmth

of the sun you can get around here (that, and those lamps for treating seasonal mood disorder). Music also helps (see 5). For extra points, purchase a reusable cup to keep it sustainable (another Seattle tradition).

3. Rain pants. Believe it or not, "rain pants" are actually an apparel category in their own right! Rain pants are basically water-repellent pants (preferably nylon) that can be worn over your regular pants to keep you dry in conditions where umbrellas just won't cut it (those Seattle days when rain just "hangs" in the air rather than "falls" from the sky). Any outdoor clothing or hiking equipment store around Seattle provides a number of variations; try to get vented, breathable ones because nylon gets rather stuffy. And if you think wearing rain pants may be a bit extreme, it sure beats sitting at your desk in a pair of rain-soaked jeans or slacks under the air-conditioning all day. The key is to fold them up and leave them in your car or messenger bag, just in case.

4. Rubber boots. Seattle pavements, upon closer inspection, are in rather bad shape—full of potholes, cracks, and dips—in many places. This is because we like to put chains on our tires whenever there's a warning of the slightest chance of snowfall in the wintertime (not actual snowfall, mind you). And everyone driving around on the raw concrete—Seattle buses included—with chains attached will ultimately result in pockmarked pavements, which in combination with heavy rain results in puddles and knee-high streams all over the streets. Rubber boots are great for keeping your feet dry, and a number of fashionable companies make them in stylish variations such as sneaker-style outsoles or Hello Kitty prints. Keep a pair of sneakers to change into in your desk drawer, and your feet will thank you on long workdays.

5. Headphones and MP3 player. Natural sunlight is known to trigger endorphins, the body's built-in mood enhancers. But with sunlight being a rare commodity in these parts, Seattle locals are finding other ways to keep themselves psyched, like "Walking on Sunshine" (great song!) when really, they just stepped into a knee-high puddle (see 4). Music glosses over the grayness and brings some color back into your life. You can make a rainy day playlist and invest in some noise-canceling headphones with nice bass lines for some "oompf" when the rest of the world goes "squish-squish." (Chocolate and spicy foods are also great ways to wring some happy chemicals out of your brain, and both are highly popular in Seattle for a good reason.)

MAJOR ATTRACTIONS

Seattle has many interesting outdoor, arts, educational, and shopping destinations. On a recent first-time visit to Seattle, I visited the following very popular tourist attractions. While there's a lot more to do and see, these represent some of the more unique options that visitors of all ages and tastes will enjoy.

PIKE PLACE MARKET

Corner of First Ave. and Pike St., Seattle, WA 98101
MON–SAT: 9:00 a.m.–6:00 p.m.
SUN: 9:00 a.m.–5:00 p.m.
(206) 682-7453
www.pikeplacemarket.org

The Pike Place Market is not hard to find. Located centrally in downtown, within walking distance of major hotels, the market is visible from blocks away because of its large, lighted sign. The indoor market features hundreds of small stalls and stands that sell fruits, vegetables, seafood, crafts, accessories, and myriad other items. Many products and goodies are specific to the Pacific Northwest, providing a quick guide to local flavors and tastes. The market is a long stretch of stalls that extends for blocks. At busy times, typically the weekends, it may take a while to traverse the length of it. But since you're likely to wander, taste, and experience some of the shops, it could easily occupy a few hours or even half a day.

Several restaurants are located in the market, which makes it very convenient to take a break from shopping to sit down for a meal. A few of these restaurants have views of the Puget Sound since the market is just a stone's throw away from the waterfront. An alternative to a typical restaurant would be one of the many of the food stands, one aspect of the market that really shines. It's quite an experience to eat-in at one of the stands in the midst of the crowd that makes its way through the market.

Visiting the market with kids is manageable but will require some patience if you visit on a weekend. The teeming crowds can overwhelm small children, depending on their temperament. But the fun and excitement children experience by seeing so many interesting crafts, toys, and other goodies is more than enough to offset the occasional crowdedness. Bathrooms are located throughout the facility.

Pike Place Market is a venerable farmers market on steroids. And luckily, it's located indoors, which means you can visit regardless of the weather.

SPACE NEEDLE

400 Broad St., Seattle, WA 98109
(206) 905-2100
www.spaceneedle.com

Most people know the Space Needle was originally built to showcase Seattle's prowess when it hosted the 1961 World's Fair. The structure, which extends 608 feet into the air, has dotted the city's skyline ever since. Surrounding the Space Needle, a number of additional tourist and learning venues have sprung up to make the area a robust itinerary for any local or visitor. The Space Needle itself features several things to do. As you might expect, this starts with an elevator ride to the top of the structure, where you can enter the observation deck. The elevator moves very quickly. As it whisks you away to the top, you may be surprised by how quickly you get there. There is a cost to make the journey. Lines are generally not a challenge—a welcome respite when compared to popular attractions in other major cities. The manageability of visiting attractions in Seattle is one very positive, recurring theme.

At the top of the structure sits a restaurant called SkyCity, which is truly unique and an experience that should not be passed up. Several features distinguish the restaurant. First, the circular restaurant literally rotates a full 360 degrees, completing an entire spin every hour. Since the restaurant is walled by windows, this allows guests to get a full panoramic view of the city and surrounding geography while enjoying a meal. The restaurant itself is well apportioned and elegantly designed. Booth seating is very comfortable, and there is sufficient room between tables. Meal prices are not cheap but not exorbitant. Look for the combination deal that includes the elevator pass with a meal. If you dine at the SkyCity restaurant at the top of the Space Needle, you will receive a complimentary elevator ride (with a minimum restaurant purchase of twenty dollars). That price also comes with free valet parking.

After completing your tour of the Space Needle, you may want to spend time in the gift shop located in the lobby. It features the standard gift items such as T-shirts, building replicas, coffee mugs, and postcards.

WASHINGTON STATE FERRIES
www.wsdot.com/ferries/schedule

The Washington State Ferries travel to islands that sit outside Seattle. One popular and very manageable trip that will take only part of a day is a visit to Bainbridge Island. The trip takes about forty-five minutes each way. Traveling on the ferries is inexpensive and comfortable. You can catch views of Seattle's waterfronts and the pure, blue waters of the Puget Sound from the upper and lower decks of the ferry. Once you arrive at the island, there's a number of fun things to do. Bainbridge Island provides a nice view of the Puget Sound, as it stares back at the city of Seattle. There are several blocks of restaurants and shops to explore once you get to the main street from a ferry station. If you have a sweet tooth, one required pit stop is Mora Ice Cream, where you can get organic ice cream. In three to four hours, you can explore the island and make the round-trip without any advance planning. Be sure to bring a jacket if you plan to sightsee on the decks, as it can get quite windy and chilly.

PACIFIC SCIENCE CENTER
200 Second Ave. N., Seattle, WA 98109
(206) 443-2001
DAILY: 10:00 a.m.–6:00 p.m.
www.pacificsciencecenter.org

Located on the same grounds as the Space Needle sits a diverse collection of science venues that are especially targeted for children. These include the planetarium, IMAX theater, and laser dome. In a half day you can visit a few of these attractions. A sample itinerary would be to catch an IMAX movie (preferably one of the 3D options), walk the floor of the center to interact with the hands-on science stations, and make your way to one of the exhibits that cover a specific topic (a current example is the butterfly house). The IMAX features educational movies, typically covering animals, space, or ocean life. The science stations cover topics like sound and sight via hands-on materials children can engage with. Exhibits that cover specific topics typically last a few weeks and take you into more detail on a particular subject matter. One such example, the butterfly exhibition, is literally a garden where you can take a stroll with butterflies of many different varieties in their natural habitat. There's no separation between the people and the butterflies, so visitors are instructed to walk slowly and gently through the small garden as butterflies fly around and occasionally land in your path. Be sure to bring your camera for close-up shots of these magnificent creatures, whose beautiful variety of colors is breathtaking. Children are instantly amazed and enamored with their time in the garden, and it's a great way to cap off a few hours learning more about nature.

If you're a bit tired after chaperoning children through all the science center has to offer, the grounds outside the science center are a good spot to rest and laze. There's ample grass to spread a picnic blanket, and children will gravitate toward the modern art structures, which they can make use of as pseudo playground.

ADVENTURES

Go Nocturnal: Late-Night Walks

As spring kicks in, I find myself out later and more often than during the earlier months. Unfortunately, our wonderful city has a few bus routes that end earlier than I like. Taxis are always an option, but I prefer to save those for when there's company needed to impress and speed's desired. And let's be honest, Seattle is a fairly safe, pretty, and interesting city. So I usually walk. And the city looks much different at night with a friendly crew of nocturnal friends waiting to meet you.

While so many Seattleites neglect the opportunities for adventure, you can create your own with a good old-fashioned drunk walk. When I was young, it was the walk from the Avenue and its brightly lit streets, then through the dark forests of Ravenna Park, which is a great shortcut as long as you aren't afraid of the dark. Emerging from the woods to the tranquil North Seattle neighborhoods around when the cherry trees are blooming is a simple pleasure few appreciate. You can take off your shoes and walk through the petals, like a prophetic figure from the past. Very soothing on your sore, worn, stumbling feet.

As I've grown older, the routes and adventures have grown and changed. The walks from Capitol Hill to the Central District have become one of my favorites. Mainly because I always miss the last bus, and I often see the sun coming up.

People often give me flak for going this route, but due to the gradual "yuppification" of Seattle, it's fine. CD is really so much safer than places like, say, Bogota at night. Believe me. I've made friends along the way, traded sips of my Andre for some gin or Hennessy, and have even been offered a sandwich or two.

I could elaborate, but my advice is this: When you end up in Queen Anne and you wanted to be in Belltown, just let your feet tell you where to go. They know adventure better than you do.

WALKING WITH GHOSTS

Seattle Ghost Tour
1410 Lower Post Alley, Seattle, WA 98101
(206) 805-0195
Tickets: $15
TUES–THURS and SUN: Departures at 5:00 p.m. and 7:00 p.m.
FRI–SAT: Departures at 5:00 p.m., 7:00 p.m., and 9:00 p.m.
www.seattleghost.com

Every city has its ghost stories, but few of them have enough to support an entire tour based around them.

That's why skeptics and believers alike will enjoy what the Seattle Ghost Tour has to offer. Rooted in the city's tragic history of the events that took place around the Great Fire in 1889, the tour begins—appropriately enough—in the basement of the Alibi Room, one of Seattle's oldest and most haunted bars. You'll learn about the mysterious figures often seen down there by employees and guests alike, and the history behind Seattle's most infamous serial killer. You'll also learn why some of Seattle's most popular nightlife spots in Post Alley will send a chill down your spine the next time you set foot inside, and ultimately why Pike Place Market is now largely known as the most haunted location in the Pacific Northwest.

Departing six nights a week from the famous Gum Wall in the market, this walking tour isn't a ghost hunt but a seventy-five-minute series of frightening stories that all take their origins from the same place—the very ground you'll be standing on. After all, the truth is stranger than fiction.

Hurricane Ridge

While many visitors to Seattle look out to the Olympic Mountains only to begin planning their "next" trip to the Northwest, few realize how close the national park is to Seattle. My family's favorite day trip out of Seattle is to Hurricane Ridge, a seventy-mile land and sea adventure to the highest elevation that one can drive to on the Olympic Peninsula.

A typical day trip to Hurricane Ridge will start out with a hearty breakfast from the famed "5 Spot" café in Queen Anne. Since the round-trip drive time to Hurricane Ridge is approximately five hours, you can afford to take your sweet time on the delicious food this place serves up. The extra "reserves" will come in handy if you plan to do any of the activities that Hurricane Ridge offers, such as snowshoeing or skiing.

After the crew gets their fill, head south to Pier 52's ferry terminal in downtown Seattle. You will take the Bainbridge Island ferry, which takes approximately forty-five minutes from departure to arrival. An alternative route can be taken via a ferry from Edmonds to Kingston. However, you will miss out on some fantastic scenery along the way. After crossing the

Puget Sound, you'll have about an hour and a half more to drive until you reach Hurricane Ridge.

Hurricane Ridge is located seventeen miles south of Port Angeles. The road that leads you up to Hurricane Ridge is open throughout the summer, and open Friday through Sunday during the winter months, weather permitting. Make sure to check the status of the road on the nps.gov Web site before visiting the park.

KIDS' ACTIVITIES

In this chapter, we have tried to outline a few suggestions for activities to do with kids (either yours or borrowed). Again, for those of us who don't get out much, these are places you'd have to start with. There are obvious activities like the zoo (what kid doesn't like staring at motionless animals while eating cotton candy?) and less obvious activities like going to Pike Place Market (do not throw fish at your toddler).

Remember, any activity can be fun, exciting, and memorable if you bring a child. Getting coffee or riding the ferry can be fraught with exhilarating moments of suspense and joy. That being said, the hope is that the list below is filled with activities that, at minimum, provide lasting memories for you and your kid.

THE CHILDREN'S MUSEUM

305 Harrison St., Seattle, WA 98109
(206) 441-1768
MON–FRI: 10:00 a.m.–5:00 p.m.
SAT–SUN: 10:00 a.m.–6:00 p.m.
thechildrensmuseum.org

A miniature world awaits all visitors to the Seattle Children's Museum. Children of all ages can act out a play at the Bijou Theatre, take a hike in the Pacific Northwest woods, and end the hike by sliding down a glacier. There are kid-sized houses from around the world to explore. The Cog City exhibit has enough levers, buttons, pulleys, tubes, labyrinths, and pipes to make physics fun. The museum is a great place for babies and toddlers to enjoy textures, sights, and sounds.

At the Storytelling Circle, children can enter a world of princes and princesses, castles, and dragons. It offers a great place to share a quiet moment amid the hustle and bustle of the fun museum atmosphere, where children can curl up and read a book, snuggle in a lily pad tent, or relax on oversized pillows. Parents can check out the books in the Parent Resource Library, with topics ranging from simple parenting tips to children's cognitive development.

Directions: The Children's Museum is located on the first level of the Center House in Seattle Center.

PACIFIC SCIENCE CENTER
200 2nd Ave. N., Seattle, WA 98109
(206) 443-2001
MON–FRI 10:00 a.m.–5:00 p.m.
SAT–SUN 10:00 a.m.–6:00 p.m.
www.pacificsciencecenter.org

There's a lot to do at the Pacific Science Center, so either plan for multiple trips or at least pack a lunch for an all-day trip. If your kids are into prehistoric reptiles, then the "Dinosaurs: A Journey Through Time" exhibit may be the place for them. The exhibit features animatronic creatures realistic enough to be almost scary. In the Tech Zone, sports enthusiasts are able to play games of virtual soccer or operate all sorts of heavy machinery to perform construction tasks. For those without the desire for virtual physical activity, the Willard Smith Planetarium shows free star shows multiple times during the week. There are two IMAX theaters that also show various films throughout the week.

Little ones can wear aprons—or not—and splash around in the water. You can also take aim at spinning and moving targets with water cannons located in the outside Fountain Court or play on a nice selection of climbing toys in the separate, walled-off toddler area. Parents can admire the white soaring arches and reflecting pools that define the unique architecture at the Pacific Science Center.

Directions: The Pacific Science Center is located in Seattle Center.

Seattle Aquarium

1483 Alaskan Way, Seattle, WA 98101
(206) 386-4300
DAILY: 9:30 a.m.–6:00 p.m.
www.seattleaquarium.org

The Seattle Aquarium isn't as large as other city aquariums, but it's quite pleasant, especially for children. Children of all ages love the seals and playful otters, as well as the giant Pacific octopus. The wet table is a thirteen-foot hands-on experience, where kids can touch rockfish, sea stars, and plankton. The wet table is also a great place to learn about tide pools and the plants and animals on the Pacific Coast. Feeding times are the most popular times to see the aquarium in action—naturalists often give short talks or training demonstrations at the same time. The most unique display is the series of demonstrations on salmon migration. The Seattle Aquarium is one of the spawning grounds of a variety of pacific salmon, with a working fish ladder and all.

Directions: The Seattle Aquarium is located on the Seattle waterfront, just west of downtown.

WOODLAND PARK ZOO

5500 Phinney Ave. N., Seattle, WA 98103
(206) 548-2500
October–April: DAILY 9:30 a.m.–4:00 p.m.
May–September: DAILY 9:30 a.m.–6:00 p.m.
www.zoo.org

The Woodland Park Zoo has been a pioneer in natural exhibition, with animals living in natural settings and habitats rather than cages. Extra space for the animals means extra walking for the humans. Kids of all ages can pet or view animals as in a typical zoo setting. They'll have a blast playing in the fun-filled indoor Zoomazium or the outdoor Habitat Discovery Loop. When it's time to eat, the Rain Forest Food Pavilion offers a range of earth-friendly and kid-friendly options, plus indoor and outdoor seating. The new west entrance contains a wonderful gift shop where the little ones can finally hug the meerkat or penguin they've wanted to all day (plush toys, of course).

Young kids will have a blast climbing and sliding at the Zoomazium, or crawling on a giant spider web and exploring caves at the Habitat Discovery Loop. The Family Farm is popular with kids because they can touch goats, rabbits, and sheep.

Kids of all ages seem to enjoy the elephants. These animals are often very active, and hard to hide—a good combination for zoo animals.

Directions: The Woodland Park Zoo is located in the Phinney Ridge neighborhood, located five miles north of downtown Seattle.

Pike Place Market

Corner of First Ave. and Pike St., Seattle, WA 98101
MON–SAT: 9:00 a.m.–6:00 p.m.
SUN: 9:00 a.m.–5:00 p.m.
(206) 682-7453
www.pikeplacemarket.org

Good for kids? Where else can you see flying fish, pig statues, and flower vendors overflowing into the aisle? Pike Place Market is one of those rare attractions that appears to be crowded with tourists and also draws the local crowd. The stalls are overflowing with crafts, gifts, jewelry, flowers, fish, meat, and seasonal produce fresh from local farms. The unique shops below ground will keep kids and grown-ups browsing for hours, and there are plenty of family-friendly lunch and dinner options. Outside you'll enjoy a fresh-air walk along the waterfront, with spectacular mountain views and the occasional ferry gliding by.

Maybe the biggest draw is the Pike Place Fish Market: order a salmon and the fishmongers toss them directly to you, sending them soaring through the air to the delight (and sometimes horror) of the crowd. Keep the kids close. Although the fishmongers are accurate, fish can be slippery. No worse way to start a tantrum than to be hit by a flying fish.

Directions: The Pike Place Market is located in downtown Seattle, close to the waterfront, on Pike Street (if you can imagine).

WASHINGTON STATE FERRY

www.wsdot.com/ferries/schedule

Washington State Ferry is the largest ferry system in the United States, serving nearly eighteen million commuters and visitors a year. Eight routes service twenty terminals, including the downtown Seattle ferry docks at Piers 50 and 52, the Fauntleroy dock in West Seattle, Bainbridge and Vashon islands, Bremerton, and others. Washington State Ferries allow passengers to experience the magnificent Puget Sound scenery, including bald eagles and sometimes orca whales and other sea life along the way. Kids and adults alike will love the adventure of driving on and off a large boat—there is something magical about riding the ferry on a summer afternoon.

The schedule changes seasonally and varies by day of the week, with adjusted schedules on holidays year round. Food service is available on some routes and can vary from boat to boat—you can always bring your own snack to enjoy on the deck of the big floating adventure.

Directions: The Washington State Ferry system operates out of downtown Seattle—obviously located on the waterfront.

PETS

Taking Your Dog Out

Seattle is one of the most pet-friendly cities in the U.S., boasting a large in-city parks and recreation system spread across its many neighborhoods. Seattle's metropolitan area is 53,178 acres, 6,189 of which are covered by parks (11.52%). Several in-city gems rank among the greatest parks in the U.S., such as the Green Lake, Gas Works, and Discovery parks. Seattle is ranked #9 in the top ten "pet-friendly" cities. Most of the cities ranked ahead of Seattle are much smaller, making it perhaps the "pet-friendliest" large metropolitan area in the country. (*Popular Science* ranks Seattle among the elite tier in a similar, wider study that ranks the "greenest" U.S. cities. This study finds Seattle to be second only to its smaller Northwestern counterpart, Portland, Oregon, when it comes to the size and quality of its parks and "green spaces.") For dog lovers in particular, Seattle has been dubbed a veritable paradise, with its combination of urban amenities and nearby outdoor attractions. Many restaurants, pubs, and even workplaces cater to dog owners, seeking to satisfy the large population of dog owners throughout the city.

Parks and Recreation

Seattle has eleven parks that are officially labeled "dog parks," as you can legally let your pet off its leash. These parks, spread throughout the city, are easily found via an Internet search. Two parks to highlight are the large Golden Gardens in Ballard and the sprawling Warren G. Magnuson on Sand Point Way. The former is situated near one of the most popular neighborhoods in the city; Ballard has become a favorite of Seattle's young, urban population. The park itself is a major attraction in Seattle, perched on Puget Sound and offering extraordinary views of the Olympic Mountains; you may witness a wedding while strolling through its grounds. The off-leash portion of the park is large and offers an opportunity to run your dog, but the rest of the park's features are enough to make the visit worth it even if you have to keep your pooch tethered. In the same vein, Warren G. Magnuson Park is a great place to spend an afternoon even if you can't let your dog off of the leash. Seattle's second-largest park has sports fields, boating, and a mile-long stretch of shoreline along Lake Washington. The park grounds cover a former naval base, offering a history lesson in Seattle's early twentieth century existence. Outside of its designated "dog parks," Seattle has over 450 park zones that can be enjoyed with your pet on its leash. Headlining this set is Green Lake Park, which has a three-mile constructed path that loops around the lake, perfect for walking a dog.

Restaurants, Pubs, and the Workplace

Several Seattle restaurateurs have tailored their businesses to attract the many Seattleites who would prefer to take their pets out with them. Every major Seattle neighborhood has at least one such pub or eatery. These establishments are indexed by several Internet directories, making them easy to find. The best of these is bringfido.com, which also rates them according to various categories for pet friendliness. Some highlights recommended by the authors are Norm's Eatery in Fremont, the Duchess in the University District, and the Seventy-fourth Street Ale House in Greenwood. For owners who don't wish to part with their pets during the workday, many large Seattle companies have adopted pet-friendly policies. Amazon.com, one of the city's largest technology firms, allows the majority of its employees stationed at the corporate headquarters to bring their dogs to work with them.

Animal Shelters

If you're looking to adopt a pet, there's no better place to look than an animal shelter. Animal shelters around the country provide for lost and abandoned animals, caring for the ailments of any in need and ensuring that their animals find healthy homes. The Seattle Animal Shelter is no exception.

The Seattle Animal Shelter offers many services that make it a great first step on your path to finding the perfect companion. They offer a large variety of pets, creating a one-stop shop for whatever friend you might be looking for. You'll find dogs, cats, rabbits, birds, reptiles, and other small mammals all looking for owners to take care of them. Animals are constantly being adopted, so you can return as often as you'd like to meet new ones. The volunteers are always happy to introduce you to the animals, allowing you to pet, hold, and play with them to find the perfect chemistry.

Furthermore, the Seattle Animal Shelter offers services beyond adoption, simplifying the adoption process for those with busy lives. They house a surgical clinic to provide spay and neuter services, and they are able to license your pet as soon as you adopt it.

While it may be easy to find a breeder online with exactly what you're looking for, you'll often find yourself adopting a pet who's been treated badly or is afflicted with an illness the owner doesn't tell you about. However, when adopting from an animal shelter, you'll receive complete medical records, assuring you that your new friend is healthy and in tip-top shape. The Seattle Animal Shelter also provides online records of the animals they currently house (including those living in temporary homes waiting for adoption), making it simple to find the perfect furry pal for your lifestyle, even if you can't make it out to visit the shelter.

In an age where the Internet provides you with so many services, including pet-finding Web sites, animal shelters still shine bright as the best place to adopt a pet. From a wide selection of species to friendly staff, an easy adoption process, and a chance to play with potential adoption candidates before choosing, you'll find that the Seattle Animal Shelter provides an intimate process for finding a playmate.

Pet-Friendly Bars

Apollo the bulldog is hoping to find a permanent life partner from the Seattle Animal Shelter someday. Until then, he frequents Seattle's dog-friendly bar scene to spend a casual evening with local pups looking for a sniff and romp while their owners enjoy a meal and a beer. His favorite watering hole is Norm's Eatery & Alehouse in the Fremont neighborhood for three main reasons:

1. When he follows the smell of sizzling burgers and melted mac 'n' cheese across the threshold between the rainy Seattle sidewalk and the comforting warmth of an indoor restaurant, no one stops him.
2. Once inside, he's welcomed by dog-loving people and other well-behaved dogs, lounging by the barstools or sitting under the tables.
3. The Thursday night combination of happy hour that goes until 7:00 p.m. and trivia that starts at 8:00 p.m. creates the perfect level of excitement and distraction that keeps the food slipping off the tables and into his belly.

Apollo and his new friend for the evening, Rufus, greet trivia players along with the official Norm's door dog.

A Guide to Seattle if You Are Stuck Inside with Your Cat

If it's too cold and rainy to go outside, your cat will probably be happy for you to stay inside and entertain it. The alternative, of course, would be for it to sit quietly or take a nap. While these are excellent ways to spend time, it is very likely that your cat already spends more time than it would like taking naps and sitting quietly while you are away. So it is best to try other activities during those moments when you are both home.

However, people don't always enjoy the same activities as cats. For example, many cats enjoy an occasional paw at the scratching post, which keeps their claws in shape and makes an appealing (to cats) sound. Humans, on the other hand, do not tend to enjoy using scratching posts and would become bored very quickly with this activity.

Therefore, it is important to focus on activities that are either enjoyable to both you and your cat or enjoyable enough for your cat that you will have fun watching it play. While it is also an option to focus only on activities you will enjoy, there are not many of these that your cat will want to watch you do, unless you enjoy watching videos of flying birds or chasing cat toys.

One activity that nearly all cats like is playing in boxes. A medium-sized box is best. Specifically, the best boxes are one and a half to two times larger than the space your cat covers when lying down. This allows sufficient room for the cat to stand, sit, or lie down in the box, which is generally its primary interest as it relates to boxes. It is also small enough that your cat will feel like it has its own space that it doesn't have to share with you or other pets. If you have hardwood floors, you can put the box on those, which will allow it to slide around as your cat jumps in and out. This creates an exciting situation for your cat because it wonders why the box moves underneath. To create an even livelier experience, you can put many boxes down and watch as your cat navigates between them. Some cats will jump from box to box, and others will belly-slide between the open flaps and the floor. But be careful when walking—who knows where your cat might be hiding?

If all else fails, you can focus on one activity that both you and your cat will be certain to enjoy together—eating. While it is likely that you enjoy different foods, cats like to have a delicious snack just as much as humans do. Experiment with different foods—you might even find something you both like!

ONLY IN SEATTLE: ECCENTRICITIES SPECIFIC TO SEATTLE

The streets of Fremont, a neighborhood in Seattle, become filled every year, the third weekend in June, with bike riders celebrating the summer solstice. Crowds gather to watch the cyclists who boast a unique style while riding their bikes...that is to say, *limited* style, as the bikers ride in the nude, at times using body paint to emphasize the brightness of the season. If you are not super enthusiastic about seeing bodies of all shapes, sizes, and ages proudly shown off, you may want to skip this particular festival...but it is indeed a one-of-a-kind spectacle! Should you choose to enjoy Fremont's peculiarities, be sure to check out the Fremont Troll during your visit. This attractive creature spends his time under Seattle's Aurora Bridge, quietly awaiting visitors...keeping a one-eyed glance on those who approach his premises. Be wary of driving near his massive stone hands, however, particularly if your car has a California license plate, as the troll has an apparent knack for grabbing these cars right from the road.

The eccentricities of Seattle continue in Fremont's neighboring town, Ballard. This area is characterized by Nordic heritage; there are numerous Scandinavian festivals throughout the year, and the town has stylish reminders of its background as well, with numerous flags and building décor. It would not be out of the ordinary to catch glimpses of kilt-wearing bagpipe players roaming the streets on sunny weekend mornings, interspersed with twenty-something-year-olds walking or running their dogs along one of Ballard's popular waterfront viewpoints.

The main purpose of the "**Ballard Locks**" (or Hiram M. Chittenden Locks) is to connect two main bodies of water: Puget Sound and Lake Washington. The water and salt levels between these two bodies of water are different, so the locks maintain these levels, while also allowing boats to cross through the area (using enclosed mechanisms that both raise and lower water levels accordingly so that boats can move through the area). In addition to watching numerous vessels move through the locks, the area also offers a prime viewing location for migrating fish. Salmon species living in the Pacific Northwest migrate back and forth between salt water and fresh water; the Ballard Locks also include a "fish ladder" that allows these fish to "jump" from one body of water to the next. Under the locks, viewing windows allow spectators to watch the fish in action.

Further out of the downtown area of Ballard, we come to **Golden Gardens**, a public park that offers a sandy beach, as well as panoramic views of beach, mountains, and area islands. The park is a favorite for summertime enthusiasts looking for the perfect location for outdoor barbecues and bonfires. A sunny day brings varied crowds to the beach: children with grandparents scrambling in tow, teenagers enjoying games of frisbee, young couples throwing sticks into the water for their dogs to retrieve. The sunshine in Seattle brings the masses outdoors, and the waterfront views in Ballard are one of the favorite native attractions.

CONVENTIONS

Some of the biggest draws in the Seattle area are the various conventions that happen throughout the year. Because there are a large number of geeks in the area, the conventions tend to reflect the interests of these groups.

One of the larger conventions in the area is **NorWesCon**. NorWesCon happens annually over Easter weekend, and it's held at the SeaTac DoubleTree hotel in SeaTac, Washington, near the airport. While this convention began with a focus on science fiction and fantasy writing, recent years have shown an expansion into various other forms of alternative lifestyles and interests. The costumes that come out of this convention are elaborate and span interests from standard TV and movie costumes to original aliens and fantastic creatures. Every year, there are special guest authors and artists, and there are several panels on different aspects of writing, along with panels on costuming, gaming, and general geek culture.

During the same weekend as NorWesCon is **SakuraCon**. SakuraCon is a more specialized convention, focusing on anime, and is held at the Washington State Convention and Trade Center. Because the focus of the convention is narrower than NorWesCon, the panels and guests tend to be more specialized, focusing on different aspects of anime and manga. There are contests for best anime music videos, fanfiction, manga, and, of course, costumes. In addition, there are rooms specifically set up for gaming, both video games and table-top board, card, and role-playing games.

Finally, speaking of games, there is **PAX**, also known as the Penny Arcade Expo. Held at the end of August, this is one of the biggest gaming conventions in North America. Only a few years old, it has grown exponentially every year and has spawned a spin-off convention called PAX East, held in Boston in March. PAX focuses on video games, but it also has a great deal of space devoted to board and role-playing games as well. Also held at the Washington State Convention and Trade Center, this convention takes over downtown Seattle as gamers from around the country show up in droves to get sneak peeks at new games coming from the biggest developers, and a chance to sit in panels to speak with these developers. There's also a fantastic games library, where any attendee can check out a board or card game and play it on-site, giving many people a chance to play games they may never have seen before.

Photo © Eric Franklin, used with permission

The conventions mentioned above are the three biggest, but they are by no means the only ones in Seattle. Multiple other conventions are held in the Seattle area every year, each with a different focus—some are meant for writers, some for game designers, and some for anyone who wants to get together with friends and hang out in costume. Overall, Seattle is a great place for bringing like-minded people together in conventions and giving them the chance to explore the interests they share.

NORTHWEST FOLKLIFE FESTIVAL

For those who do not have the interest or money to join the mass exodus from Seattle to the pop music festival Sasquatch in central Washington every Memorial Day weekend, Seattle Center is the site of the people's festival of music and culture: the **Northwest Folklife Festival**. Gathering for its fortieth year in 2011, the Northwest Folklife Festival (often simply referred to by locals as "Folklife") is a four-day celebration of the diversity and creativity of everyday life in the Pacific Northwest. Featuring six thousand performers and a volunteer operations staff of eight hundred, the Northwest Folklife Festival attracts about 250,000 visitors over the four-day weekend, making it one of the largest *free* community festivals in the United States.

Through community-curated events and stages, along with a wide variety of impromptu opportunities to participate in dance, music, food, and art, festivalgoers are treated to an incredible range of creativity and cultural expression right in their own backyard—and the close juxtaposition of cultures is quite often remarkable. Baby boomer old-time fiddlers mingle with teenaged eight-bit computer rockers; Polynesian practitioners of hula convene with Sephardic Jewish clarinetists; cowboys demonstrate cooking with a Dutch oven over a campfire while Thai chefs prepare their traditional foods in a wok. And everywhere you go, the sounds of the hippie drum circles are never far.

Founded in 1971, Northwest Folklife was formed as a non-profit organization largely staffed by volunteers charged with producing a regional folklife festival in collaboration with what is now the National Council on the Traditional Arts. In the early years, the Northwest Folklife Festival featured revivalist arts and crafts popular with the regional counterculture of the day, with a strong emphasis on Anglo-American traditional music and dance.

In the 1980s, a professional staff was developed to broaden the scope of the organization's mission, reaching out to involve and engage a wider range of Pacific Northwesterners and expressing that diversity through its programming. In the 1990s, Northwest Folklife solidified its place within the Seattle public arts landscape, creating year-round cultural events as well as documentary media, publications, and recordings. In recent years, a stronger programming effort has been made to reach out to youth culture in the Pacific Northwest, highlighting and celebrating the traditions of DIY music, arts, and culture in the region with great success. With long-term support of the Seattle Center, King County's 4Culture, and the City of Seattle Office of Arts & Cultural Affairs, the Northwest Folklife Festival continues into its fourth decade with strength and vitality.

DRIVING IN SEATTLE

Only in Seattle is the turn signal an aftereffect. As if to answer the inevitable question of the car behind, "Where did you come from?" I've often even seen drivers use the opposite turn signal (the left signal after moving from the right lane) as if to say, pointing, "from over there."

Now I realize there are bad drivers everywhere, but Seattle has its own breed. I've driven up and down and across the country. Seattle drivers can't merge (as is typical in most places).

Also get rid of any previous notion you had of "slow," "fast," or "passing" lanes. A typical snapshot of a three-lane highway in Seattle will have a car going 40 mph in the "passing" lane, a car going 55 mph in the "fast" lane, and another car going 70 mph in the "slow" lane. This does not mean that if you use the center lane to pass the 40 mph car in the left lane, you won't get a dirty look. It just means you should drive alert. Changing speeds and lanes in Seattle is not something you can predict.

Seattle drivers drift instead of making a decisive change of lanes. This is how they show their passive-aggressive nature through their automobiles. Of course, following up the drift with an explanatory turn signal, as discussed above, makes the encounter "polite."

The last thing I'll mention as a tangent to driving in Seattle is parking in Seattle. Now I know most people don't park illegally on purpose, but be extra careful in Seattle. Ninety-eight percent of cars parked illegally *will get a ticket*. The parking patrols here are some of the best in the world. Save yourself the heartbreak when thinking you are above the law or have found a great spot or it's only five minutes; you aren't and you didn't and that's long enough. Typically, parking structures are only slightly more expensive and worth the money. There is never free parking in Seattle.

While Seattle drivers have their quirks, once you get to where you're going you will have a great time. Take some time in the passenger seat if you can (public transportation here is excellent), and take in the gorgeous mountains.

SHOPPING

QUEEN ANNE

Under the shadow of the famous Space Needle, to the north you will find quiet Queen Anne with its exquisite set of boutique shops. If you are looking for a gift for kids, parents, or that special someone, look no further.

Meadow offers you a wide range of accessories and home decoration products at sensible prices. Always be prepared to have extra space in the trunk once you are here. At **Fox's Gem** shop, you will find courteous and helpful people who help you pick the perfect gem. You don't just shop here. You build a relationship that will bring you back for more.

Other shops like **Florentia Clayworks** with its exquisite interior clay decors, **Stuhlberg's Inc., Once Upon a Time** with their unique and affordable kids sections, and **Pink Ginger**, a charming women's boutique, promise the wonderful shopping experience you are looking for.

Parking is a breeze in this locality, and it is well connected to the freeways.

UNIVERSITY DISTRICT

Just north of downtown Seattle, bustling with college kids and a lot of purple and gold, is the University District. Known for being home to the University of Washington, it is also a great place to find fabulous, trendy pieces or great vintage outfits. University Avenue, or "The Ave." to locals, is a few blocks from the University of Washington campus and is full of places eat, study, grab coffee, or *shop*. There is **Pitaya**, a women's clothing store where you can go to get a good idea of what is in style at the moment. It is fairly inexpensive, and with a variety of items from summer dresses to trendy tops to handbags, Pitaya is the perfect place to find a great outfit you won't find many other people wearing.

If vintage is more your style, head over to **Red Light Vintage and Costume**, where you can find fun, funky items. It is the perfect place to find a costume for any occasion. The Ave. is also home to stores like **Urban Outfitters, Aprie,** and **American Apparel**. If you want to find Husky gear, the Ave. is your spot; from **The Dawg Den** to **The University Book Store**, you will be sure to find purple and gold attire.

Just down the hill from University Avenue is an outdoor mall called **University Village**. There is a wide variety of shops in University Village from clothing chains such as **The GAP, Banana Republic, Tommy Bahama,** and **H&M** to home-decoration stores like **Crate and Barrel** and **Pottery Barn. Fireworks** is a unique and inviting store that has a great variety of gift items and fun things for your home. **Mercer** is a women's clothing store unique to the Seattle area that has an array of denim in a variety of styles and washes plus great tops. University Village is such a fun place to shop and has so many great stores to visit; it shouldn't be missed on any trip to Seattle.

CAPITOL HILL

While Capitol Hill may not be a shopping epicenter when compared to downtown Seattle in terms of a vast selection of name-brand stores, the unique and vibrant neighborhood has a variety of gems tucked away worth exploring. The shopping experience in Capitol Hill allows you to slow down, as it is far removed from the hustle and bustle of the inner city. Even though there are fewer shoppers on a typical day than in downtown Seattle, one drawback is a lack of parking. When you find that coveted parking spot, leave the car behind and meander through the streets to find your favorite hidden gems.

To make up for the lack of parking, Capitol Hill offers a plethora of eateries interspersed between retail outlets, which will help keep your energy high as you walk from shop to shop.

SHOPPING FROM HOME

The thing about shopping in Seattle is that getting your nice, dry, cozy, warm-slippered self to whichever mall or store you've chosen often involves going outside, where you will likely be exposed to rain, wind, cold, and—God forbid—other people. Do you think they're in a good mood once they're all wind-blown and rain-soaked? They are not. And what about leaving once you've purchased your bounty, arms loaded down with packages that, once wet, could disintegrate in your arms, leaving a trail of your treasures all the way back to your car? Think that's your only problem? Is your hair done? It won't be when you're finished. Therefore, I've found shopping online to provide perfect respite against the elements.

Shopping online these days is perfectly safe, exposes you to a vast selection, and shipping speed and costs, if any, outweigh any need to leave the comfort of your favorite surroundings. Gas is ridiculously expensive, parking can be difficult to find and expensive if you're downtown, and don't forget about windshield wiper blades and fluid replacement costs...did I mention that it's going to rain?

Search engines like Bing.com and Google.com can help you find something you're looking for, once you know what that is. But what fun is that? Shopping is sometimes about the hunt, the kill, and the thrill of finding exactly what you needed but weren't even looking for on the day you didn't yet know you needed it. I like to be seduced into my purchases and made to think that I and I alone benefitted from my impeccable timing that perfectly coincided with the available selection and sale. To me, it's about frivolous-but-necessary thrifty bargains presented on a stick that I cannot live another day without.

And so, I'm about to introduce you to my top three choices for online shopping. If done right, you will have time to accomplish other things in your day and still get home in time to watch the weathermen lie to you about the upcoming day's forecast—something like, partly sunny, partly cloudy, chance of showers, with some afternoon clearing, with temperatures somewhere between miserably cold and generally unpleasant. Of course, this is only true ten months of the year. Those other two months are over 72 degrees, so all of Seattle will be moaning about the heat. Who wants to go out in that?

Anyway, let's get started:

Amazon.com

1. Go straight to "Today's Deals" to see what you might be missing and not know about that is on sale for a terrific price.
2. Purchase.
3. Check out the recommendations for what other people purchased who just bought this deal. (They know what they're talking about.)
4. Repeat step 2.

Tip: Make sure you're a Prime subscriber so you are assured of the instant gratification of receiving your purchase within two days. Want it sooner? Can't beat $3.99 per item for one-day shipping.

Gilt.com

1. Set your smartphone for a 9:00 a.m. PST alarm.
2. Go to Gilt and select Men, Women, Children, Home, or Gifts from which to shop.
3. Purchase any of these items that are hot, haute, and (at least for the Women's section) look fantastic on all the size 2, 5' 10" models flaunting them. They're usually a great deal, and the return policy has improved, so go crazy.
4. The home section has some great finds, and they don't require you to be in fantastic shape like you were when you were a twelve-year-old boy.

Myhabit.com

1. This is the perfect solution for fashionistas who love Amazon's fantastic shipping and who love a great deal

on high-fashion clothing and accessories for women, men, and children.

2. Shop anytime, but they also begin their best offerings at 9:00 a.m. PST. See how efficient this all is?

3. Buy with abandon, and don't think twice. If it doesn't fit and you can't re-gift it, you usually get twenty-one days to return it and receive an Amazon gift card which may be used on Myhabit.com, Amazon.com, or Endless.com, subject to the terms and conditions of the Amazon.com gift card.

Made in the USA
Lexington, KY
12 February 2014